UNTHINKING
FAITH AND ENLIGHTENMENT

Nature and the State in
a Post-Hegelian Era

JANE BENNETT

NEW YORK UNIVERSITY PRESS
New York *and* London

Library of Congress Cataloging-in-Publication Data

Bennett, Jane, 1957–
   Unthinking faith and enlightenment.

   Includes bibliographies and index.
   1. Enlightenment. 2. Faith and reason. 3. Nature.
4. Environmental policy. 5. State, The. I. Title.
B802.B445   1987   320'.01'1   87–7709
ISBN 0–8147–1095–6

Book design by Laiying Chong.

Unthinking Faith and Enlightenment

For
Don, Connie, Sue, *and* Donnie

CONTENTS

PREFACE

This is not a book about Hegel. It does examine his account of the dialectic of Enlightenment, exploring why the debate between "faith" and "pure insight" reached an impasse where neither could sustain its position without drawing illicitly from the other. To delineate this early modern debate is, I argue, to enhance comprehension of the frame in which contemporary debates over environmentalism and the state are set. And this comprehension helps us, especially after the collapse of Hegel's own solution to the impasse he diagnosed, to unthink the terms of contemporary debates and to create space for new alternatives.

I would like to thank Jean Elshtain, George Kateb, and Jerome King for their thoughtful readings of earlier drafts of the manuscript and for their many helpful comments. Kathy Ferguson introduced me to political theory as an undergraduate and I appreciate the intellectual sustenance she continues to provide. I am grateful also to Michael Shapiro for reading and rereading the manuscript and particularly for his suggestion that I draw out the rhetorical dimension of the texts I discuss. Michael Gibbons, Dwight Kiel, Charlene Stinard, and Dennis Wakefield deserve thanks for exploring these and related themes with me over the last several years. Finally, I owe a special debt to William Connolly whose advice and criticisms have been of great value to me at every stage of this project.

THE QUEST FOR A HOME

> German philosophy as a whole—Leibniz, Kant, Hegel, Schopen-
> hauer, to name the greatest—is the most fundamental form of
> romanticism and homesickness there has ever been . . .
>
> Nietzsche

HEGEL was homesick. And he evokes the sentiment in each of us. He sought to reconcile the self to its world: to locate faith inside rationality, to reunite humans with nature, to overcome estrangement from culture, to incorporate the particular into the universal. It seems impossible to arrange such a homecoming in the modern age, for the traditional synthesis of self and world has been dismantled in a self-conscious project of enlightenment. The Hegelian ontology of *Geist* provides an index to the severe obstacles facing the modern quest for a home. A heroic ontology was required to fulfill an impossible dream.

Hegel's *Phenomenology of Spirit* was the means through which the harmony of self and world was to be achieved. It was to draw the reader through the understandings necessary for absolute consciousness, the explicit recognition that one's identity was none other than universal spirit. But while there are many who appreciate Hegel's psychological, epistemological, aesthetic, political, and religious insights, no one today defends the ontology of *Geist*.

Hegel failed to harmonize human needs with the way of the world. But by helping us to see what would be required for this harmony, he contributes unwittingly to a thesis he sought to defeat: the homecoming cannot be arranged, for there is no set of philosophical or political or psychological conditions where the fit between self and world will be neat.

The quest for a home assumes that the object of the quest, a place of meaning in a meaningful universe, is the birthright of human beings. Within the terms of this quest, homesickness is a technical problem. That is to say, it is indicative of a flaw in this or that conceptual, political, or religious scheme. But the demise of Hegel's grand scheme calls into question the end for which these schemes are to be means. One begins to suspect that the quest for a home actually fosters the experience of exile—for to be "exiled" is to insist that there is a homeland to which one could in principle return and to which one rightfully belongs.

But many are not yet suspicious enough on this score. The quest for a home remains at the root of many contemporary political debates, where beneath apparent opposition often lies a shared faith that harmonious reconciliation is possible and desirable, that alienation can be transcended in this world or the next. Here Hegel's contribution to this study is a witting one. His account in the *Phenomenology* of two competing designs for homecoming, "Faith" and "Enlightenment," helps to illuminate the framework of these political debates.

In chapter 1, I offer a reading of Hegel's dialectic of Faith and Enlightenment. Enlightenment is a philosophically informed way of life that builds its home through mastery of a disenchanted world; Faith seeks meaning and comfort through partial reenchantment of the world. But, Hegel argues, neither mode can integrate self and world successfully.

Enlightenment demands a knowledge certain of itself, and lacks the resources to achieve it; it views reason as a tool for rendering the world predictable, and understates the contribution the world itself would have to make to a fully rational order; it sees nature as a deposit of resources for potential human use, and underplays the need for human implication in a world larger than itself. Faith, the defensive voice in this dialectic, strives to appreciate the mystery surrounding human knowing, and depreciates the essential link between self-consciousness and freedom; it resists the spread of instrumental rationality, and underestimates the need for technology and administration; it seeks attunement to nature, and exaggerates its providence.

In Hegel's dialectic of Faith and Enlightenment we discern recurring discursive themes: a questioning of the status of language and knowledge, an ambivalence about rationality and utilitarian social control.

Although Faith and Enlightenment expose debilitating flaws in each other, neither is able to transcend the theoretical and practical difficulties in its own affirmative position. Faith and Enlightenment engender each other; each is formed in contrast to its opponent and through recognition of its opponent's defects. Hegel argues that debates conforming to the Faith-Enlightenment dynamic will arrive at an impasse—until they accept the resolution inscribed in his impossible solution.

In chapters 2 and 3 I explore the environmental debate and the debate surrounding the theory of the state as two contemporary manifestations of the Faith-Enlightenment problematic. This exploration enables me to rethink the sources and effects of the quest for a home. What is the fallout of the project of homecoming? What are the political, moral, and existential effects of trying today to establish a home in the world? Is it possible to renounce the quest?

In each of these contemporary debates, one side emphasizes the human role in the constitution of self and world: homecoming requires a strenuous exertion of rational will, a thorough mastery of the world. The other side accentuates the order hidden within nature: reconciliation of self and world requires an attunement of human will to natural structure. These contemporary disputants reenact the earlier impasse between Faith and Enlightenment.

I argue that while the first, enlightened position exaggerates the power of human reason and will, the second, full of faith, exaggerates the beneficence of natural order. Both overestimations result in an inability to acknowledge the "otherness" within self and within nature that declines to attend any reunion. To rail against that which escapes unification with insistent attempts at humanization (as Enlightenment does) has been destructive politically, psychologically, and ecologically. But the reconstitution of otherness into the mysterious dimension of a world designed in our best interest (as in Faith) is increasingly hard to believe; it cuts too much against the grain of contemporary experience.

My aim is not to prove that contemporary discourse must be enclosed within the Faith-Enlightenment problematic—that is only one of the more important interpretive frameworks of contemporary political discourse. Rather, my intention is to reveal dimensions of these debates normally unthematized when the parameters within which they are contained are ignored.

In chapter 2, "Environmental Management and Natural Holism," I find that the orientations to nature within the contemporary environmental debate fall into two groups: environmental management, with its enlightened faith in the susceptibility of nature to technical mastery; and natural holism, with its emphasis on the interconnectedness of self and nature, on the presence of a home already beneath our feet waiting to be recognized.

Environmental management, as exemplified by economists Allen Kneese and Charles Schultze, environmental lawyer Christopher Stone, and ethicist John Passmore, gives primacy to human reason and will. Natural holism, as exemplified by natural philosophers Erazim Kohak and John Compton, gives special status to nature, conceiving it as a moral guide for human conduct.

Environmental management and natural holism are opponents intimately involved with each other, and this intimacy confines the debate between them. According to natural holism, environmental management is incapable of realizing environmental quality, for its Promethean orientation to nature is at base destructive. According to environmental management, natural holism is utopian, for it evades the necessity of a Promethean orientation by fantasizing about the extent to which self and nature can be as one.

Although the charges each makes against the other are on target, neither solution is satisfactory. Chapter 2 thus establishes an agenda to be pursued in chapter 4: the articulation of an orientation to nature more tenable than natural holism and less Promethean than environmental management.

The organization of chapter 3, "The Juridical State, the Consensual State, the Attuned State," is more complex, for Enlightenment theories of the state present both an individualist and a collectivist face. I examine the work of three contemporary theorists of the state—Theodore Lowi, Jürgen Habermas, and Charles Taylor—focusing on the link between a conception of the state and a conception of freedom. Lowi and Habermas, disagreeing on much, nonetheless share the Enlightenment inheritance and conceive political freedom as rational mastery of the natural and social worlds; Taylor protests against these two faces of Enlightenment, arguing that freedom requires respect for the "natural bent" of the self and the world. Lowi and Habermas advocate masterful agencies of power—even though each locates this power differently—with an increasing realm of responsibility, while Taylor argues for a more decentralized steady state.

The focus of the Habermasian attack on Lowi's ideal state is that its commitment to capitalism undermines its commitment to democracy. From the perspective of Taylor, however, Habermas and Lowi share an exaggerated confidence in the ability of human reason to order individuals, collectivities, or nature. This overconfidence leads both, even against their wills, to define their objects more and more in terms of use value and to enlarge the scope of social rationalization. But, again, I argue that while Taylor's critique is on target his alternative presupposes a social ontology too close to Hegel's and too detached from the world we experience.

One aim of chapter 3 is to elucidate the connection between orientations to nature and conceptions of freedom. An orientation to nature enables some conceptions of freedom and disables others. It helps to decide, for example, whether human freedom is understood as requiring transcendence of natural boundaries or acceptance of them. The orientation to "external" nature also has implications for the treatment of elements of human nature that are troublesome or resistant to reason. Because the natural environment is, in a sense, the paradigmatic "other," an approach to external nature helps to constitute the range of ethical or not-so-ethical orientations to otherness within the self.

Chapters 2 and 3 expose inconsistencies and anomalies in Faith and Enlightenment as contemporary modes of political discourse. Hegel's *Phenomenology*, by relentlessly exposing flaws in many other modern theories of self, morality, freedom, and nature, inadvertantly warns against *any* theory that seeks harmony, mastery, completion, unity. It recommends a more tentative political and theoretical stance.

In chapter 4, "Unthinking Faith and Enlightenment," I seek such a stance, one that places its faith neither in human mastery nor in a world predisposed to human needs. It seeks a political theory that acknowledges dissonance between humans and the world while appreciating our interdependence with it. It is alert to a casualty of the search for a home in the world: the "other," the self or part of the self that does not live up to standards built into the dreams of rationality or attunement. Friedrich Nietzsche and Michel Foucault inspire this ethical attempt, although they are not the authors of it.

In this final chapter I explore the environmental problem and the theory of the state from the perspective of "fractious holism." This perspective strives to acknowledge the integrity of intractable elements in the self and in the world. More important, it seeks a politics and an ethics that appreciate the world's resistance to human ordering while recognizing the indispensability of the human imperative to order.

Perhaps it is time to think past the familiar opposition in which the world is either an order of being or an intersubjective product of humanity. If it is time to transcend these alternatives, we must unthink Faith and Enlightenment.

CHAPTER 1
FAITH AND ENLIGHTENMENT

What Is Enlightenment?

THE eighteenth-century Enlightenment sought to demystify the world according to faith, where nature was God's text, filled with divine signs, intrinsic meaning, and intelligible order. In the face of belief in an enchanted cosmos, the Enlightenment sought to push God to a more distant social location; in the face of unreflective allegiance to tradition, it sought self-determination and self-conscious reason; in the face of a view of knowledge as mysterious divine hints, it sought a transparent, certain science; in the face of a sacralized nature, it sought a fund of useful natural resources.

The Enlightenment is an eighteenth-century movement, but Enlightenment is also a mode of consciousness—a set of understandings, a lived philosophy, an orienting complex of beliefs, assumptions, and presuppositions about self and world. Hegel employs the term in both the historical and the philosophical sense. Enlightenment as a mode of consciousness found its purest expression in the philosophes of the eighteenth century, but it transcends the bounds of that century. Today, to call something "modern" is frequently to invoke its Enlightenment characteristics.

According to Hegel, the self-consciousness and assertiveness of the Enlightenment were infectious: a counter-Enlightenment would have to be more reflective than the mode of consciousness the Enlightenment had demystified. A new version of Faith would have to speak in a more sophisticated, albeit more defensive, voice. And it often did. Post-Enlightenment Faith protested against the reduction of reason to instrumental rationality; it criticized the ideal of transparent knowledge by insisting that knowledge was limited by the finitude of the mind; it exposed the incompatibility of Enlightenment utilitarianism and respect for persons; it stood witness for the interdependence of humans and nature, demanding that nature be respected even if it could not be read as a text.

Enlightenment defines itself by reference to its adversary; its self-image is destroyer of myths and archaic social institutions. It applies its critique of the robust version of Faith to the modern version as well. Enlightenment exposes, in the cold light of reason, the foundation of the new Faith's moral claims as the same old religion or teleology that supplied the moral power of the Faith of an enchanted world. Faith also defines itself by reference to its adversary, however, and it too has success in its critique. It persistently exposes the narrowness, overconfidence, and contradictions within Enlightenment's exaltation of the rational, autonomous self.

The structure of my exploration of Hegel's dialectic of Faith and Enlightenment is as follows:

I begin with an account of what a more robust version of Faith might have looked like, for the Faith Hegel describes in *Phenomenology of Spirit* has already been infiltrated by Enlightenment categories. This account allows me to accentuate some of the distinctive elements of the theories of knowledge, language, self, and nature of Faith. Robust Faith is, like Faith and Enlightenment, an ideal type. The mode of consciousness I call Robust Faith does not exhaust the history preceding the Enlightenment but it establishes a space for itself prior to the Enlightenment that cannot be recaptured later. It is a construct that is to function as a set of illuminating contrasts to modern orientations. My discussion of Robust Faith ends with an argument about its self-destructive potential. Here I use Hans Blumenberg to address the question: Why is it the weakened Faith of the *Phenomenology* that endures and not a more robust version?

The chapter ends with a summary of the dialectic of Faith and Enlightenment. Faith, struggling to articulate insights that increasingly are seen as problematic, is both a target of Enlightenment's critique and a critique of Enlightenment, the mode of consciousness in ascendancy. After working through Hegel's dialectic, many contemporary debates appear as heirs to the incestuous debate between Faith and Enlightenment.

An Enchanted World

Faith in its purest expression is consistent with an enchanted view of the world,[1] where nature is filled with mystery and meaning and where each thing in nature is interconnected with every other. The world is a creation, a vast web whose threads are those of resemblance. This similitude of each with all is an ontological likeness due to the divine source of all creation—all being is linked by this deep "blood tie"—but particular things are especially close. These immediate relatives are linked by physical proximity or natural affinity (e.g., moss on trees, ticks on dogs, plants and the sun), or analogousness and complementarity of function or form. Consider Paracelsus who believes that just as the firmament with all its constellations forms a whole in itself, likewise man is a free and mighty firmament: "The sun can shine through a glass, and fire can radiate warmth through the walls of the stove, although the sun does not pass through the glass and the fire does not go through the stove; in the same way, the human body can act at a distance while remaining in one place. . . ."[2]

Knowledge in this enchanted world is organized around the principle of resemblance, but resemblance is not an *epistemology* or a conceptual scheme deployed to investigate a physical world—it is a property inherent in nature. Nature speaks and says that it coheres through relations of resemblance. Every rock, every plant reveals part of its meaning, tells what it is, and its truth is the purpose it serves in the order of creation.

There exists a sympathy between aconite and our eyes. This unexpected affinity would remain in obscurity if there were not some signature on the plant, some mark, some word, as it were, telling us that it is good for diseases of the eye. This sign is easily legible in its seeds: they are tiny dark globes set in white skinlike coverings whose appearance is much like that of eyelids covering an eye.[3]

Knowledge consists of an approximate recovery of divine intentions embodied in the natural world and revealed in signs. Nature speaks, but by necessity something is lost in the translation; nature cannot pronounce an unambiguous directive. God provides only hints, or rather, his intentions must appear to mortals as cryptic clues. This opaqueness is not only a result of the limits of human reason but is also bound up with the temporality and finitude of material things. Nature whispers therefore, but the whisper only concentrates our attention, draws our ears even closer, enhances the appeal of that which speaks.

Knowledge must have an element of mystery, for were it unambiguous, humans would have no role to play. More precisely, humans would cease to be mortal and instead become divine, because in an enchanted world the only being with access to unambiguous knowledge is God. Like every part of creation, humanity is an integral part of the ordered universe, a universe that includes the "objects" of human knowledge. Humanity is related to these objects precisely in its office as interpreter of them. The relation between humans and the world—that is, knowledge—consists then in interpretation; interpretation makes audible the world's voice.

Moreover, the veiled messages in nature are susceptible to a range of interpretations. The truth is gleaned only through multiple, partial attempts, and even the final compilation of interpretations can only approximate truth. The range is not infinite, however, for the messages are grounded and the interpretations bounded by real divine intentions—even while this ground and these limits are not fully transparent to humans.

Writings and speech in an enchanted world are like any other naturally appearing thing. Language does not function as a medium privileged by its proximity to humanity; language has not yet become—as it will after the Enlightenment—a richer mine of truth than a neutralized natural "environment." Language, like nature, is simply another site where resemblances connect earthly existence to the divine cosmos. Ancient texts, contemporary writings, theological treatises, ravings of the mad, art, music, and miracle plays were all subject to constant and relentless commentary, for overlapping interpretations were required to reveal the oracle within texts. All varieties of commentaries were encouraged: those that elaborated shape, structure, mythical history, medicinal application, smell, likenesses to other things, potential, tendencies, accidental or necessary events associated with the thing, and so forth. More important, "none of these forms of discourse is required to justify its claim to be expressing a truth before it is interpreted; all that is required of it is the possibility of talking about it."[4] The oracular nature of the text is not a specific divine command to be translated into human practice. Language does not here "represent" some real content in the world, but rather

words group syllables together and syllables letters, because there are virtues placed in individual letters that draw them towards each other or keep them apart, exactly as the marks found in nature also repel or attract one another.[5]

It is the secret workings of these movements, more than a designative message (human or divine), that commentaries tirelessly seek.

Historians have had difficulty explaining the coexistence, in the early Renaissance, of magic or divination (used to cull meaning from nature) and scholarly erudition (used to examine the rediscovered Greek and Roman texts). The former is often viewed as an element of superstition incongruous with the theoretical strides made in the field of textual exegesis. But these two forms can be seen as more than complementary. As integral parts of the epistemic configuration of a robust Faith, divination and textual commentary are methods appropriate to the production of an incomplete knowledge that is in turn appropriate to a world filled everywhere with divine hints of meaning. The model for reading nature is the same as that for reading texts. "God is revealed in Scripture; his works are also visible in the world. . . . The book of nature becomes a commentary, further substantiation of the truth of the revealed word."[6]

Just as a poet conveys a message through the medium of words (a medium that precludes the possibility of a transparent transmission) and just as it is the reader's job to participate in reconstituting a message, the author of the world speaks through signs inscribed in the world; the human role is to interpret those signs. It now becomes clear how the question of truth presented itself. For those of an enchanted world, it is unnecessary to demand the title to authority of interpretations of natural signs or texts, for God was the guarantor of their truth. Both commentary and divination possess

an ageless affinity with the things that [they] . . . unveil. . . . The truth of all these marks—whether they are woven into nature itself or whether they exist in lines on parchment . . .—is everywhere the same: coeval with the institution of God.[7]

The multiple human discourses on nature were discourses on a single, unified text, the uni-verse.

Things hide themselves in nature and the word but then offer themselves up for interpretation. The world is recalcitrant but not silent. Human knowledge or science could "bear witness" to some truth but cannot "indicate causes and effects."[8] In this form of knowing, conceptual relationships are loose but secure, both flexible and strong, more like family resemblances than efficient causes.

Let us review the orientations that are consistent with a world of Robust Faith.

(1) *Holism.* The universe is designed in a coherent and purposeful way. Each part of the whole is interconnected to every other through relations of resemblance. The earthly world is a microcosm of the order of the universe. The category "microcosm"

provides all investigations with an assurance that everything will find its mirror and its macrocosmic justification on another and larger scale; it affirms, inversely, that the visible order of the highest spheres will be found reflected in the darkest depths of the earth.[9]

(2) *Incompleteness.* Knowledge is relational—to know is to discern the authentic links between persons and their world and among things that coexist in the world. But all relations have a necessary element of opacity or mystery; knowledge can be certain or, rather, secure, without having to be complete.

(3) *Interpretation.* Knowledge is therefore interpretation. Although an enchanted world is a microcosm, the human relation to it is not completely given or rigidly fixed—it is the role of the self to participate in forming that relation through interpretation.

This characterization of Robust Faith is designed to draw a sharp contrast between modern understandings about the self, knowledge, and nature and those of an enchanted world. Compared to our world, a world that could be read like prose is integrated and harmonious, comforting and secure. But even according to my selective picture of pre-Enlightenment modes of understanding and even for the most ardent seekers of similitudes, the cosmos was a puzzle with a few pieces still missing. For example, language expressed God's intentions but remained in essence a defiled version of them. In general, all signs were imperfect indicators of truth—resemblances could never fully overcome the distance between self and other, between human and thing, between body and soul.

What is the significance of this conclusion? On one reading, the imperfect character of the signs in an enchanted world is evidence that nature does not fit the creationist mold imposed upon it: humans posited telos and divine intentionality in nature, they did not "discover" it there. The ambiguity of resemblances calls the schema of world-as-text itself into question, exposing the schema as a human construct in the service of the quest for a home. The quest prompts an ontology designed to show that the universe is essentially already a home. On another reading, the opacity of (some) signs and the (apparent) absence of others are necessary because of the limits to material and mortal being; illegible passages and missing pages are not threats to the integrity of the text if one has faith in a divine author in possession of the complete edition.

Nevertheless, an effort, a sort of deliberate naiveté, is required to sustain the second reading and to prevent the comforting mysteries of creation from becoming troublesome irrationalities in the world. And when this effort fails—as it is bound to at times, given the human capacity for self-consciousness and the skepticism it engenders—the human reader will become estranged from the comological text. Robust Faith, then, is an inherently precarious mode of consciousness: its vision of a tranquil and orderly cosmos has a tendency to blur; the depth of the tranquility and the tenability of mysterious explanations are called into question by a muted but resilient form of reflection that works to unmask resemblances. The potential for the characteristically modern experience of estrangement resides even within an enchanted world.

Hegel and Robust Faith

Hegel's characterization of an enchanted world emphasizes this alienating potential. In the *Philosophy of History* he describes three periods in the history of religion: "Christendom" where the Church/ State split is as yet undifferentiated, "feudalism" where the antithesis between a theocratic Church and a monarchical State develops, and the "Reformation" which begins the harmonization of religion and reason. The ways of thinking I have described as Robust Faith are characteristic of the first two periods which, according to Hegel, constitute "the long, eventful and terrible night" before the dawning of a re-formation of religious consciousness.

An opulent world bloated with miracles and magic was at odds with reason and self-consciousness, thus the periods of Christendom and feudalism are marked by radically insufficient modes of understanding, mere moments of a yet-to-be-realized synthesis. Consciousness was able to make certain categorical distinctions but unable to conceptualize the relation between them. This can be seen most clearly, says Hegel, in the lack of integration between "the sacred" and "the secular." The only institution capable of achieving this precarious, complex and differentiated integration is the State, in Hegel's special use of the term. But Christendom and feudalism invested reconciliatory hopes in the Church.

And the Church failed to effect a true unity of sacred and secular and instead only contaminated each realm with the worst aspects of the other. The sale of indulgences and ecclesiastical office, for example, corrupted spiritual insights with the hunger for power and wealth and corrupted everyday life with religious fear and superstition. The Church failed also because its (hypocritical) focus on chastity, poverty, and obedience was at odds with the needs of social and economic life. Marriage, the basic unit of social structure, was deemed inferior to celibacy; "pauperism, laziness, inactivity, was regarded as nobler" than activity where "the workman has to perform for his subsistence";[10] the call for blind obedience to Church doctrine violated true political freedom, "obedience . . . to the Moral and Rational . . . , to laws which I recognize as just."[11]

This last point is important. The robust faith of Christendom and feudalism did not subject belief to sufficiently critical reflection. The development of reflective conscience and individual self-consciousness was stunted by the overwhelming presence of the Church as institutional conscience. "Man, as such, is declared incapable of recognizing the Divine and approaching thereto."[12]

Nevertheless, the Church's struggle to present divinity "as not in any sense an other-world existence, but as in unity with Human Nature in the Present and Actual,"[13] drew ordinary believers to the project. These robust believers became preoccupied, says Hegel, with this question: *In what way* is the sacred made "present" and "actual," that is, sensual? The doctrine of the Trinity was the officially prescribed answer, "but when it is once granted that God exists in external phenomenal presence, this external manifestation immediately becomes infinitely varied; for the need of this presence is infinite."[14]

The significant point is that once Robust Faith was committed to the view that the spiritual has a sensual expression, it became difficult to confine the instances of this expression to those authorized by the Church. Why, for example, did the spiritual mingle in the material only in the Eucharist? Was it not possible that God provided instances of this commingling within our selves or within nature? For Hegel, it was an excessive and unauthorized enthusiasm for realizing the unity of human and divine that allowed nature to become filled with miracles.

The Church was unable to establish the hegemony of its theological explanation of the unity of human and divine—the doctrine of the Trinity. Ordinary religious consciousness had tenuous ties to this complex official doctrine and instead improvised its own:

Thus innumerable instances will occur . . . in which Christ has appeared to one and another, in various places. . . . In all places . . . there will occur manifestations of the Heavenly . . . and the Divine will be realized in *miracles*.[15]

Unable to restrain or channel this zealousness for unity on the part of the believers, the Church eventually incorporated an enchanted view of nature into its own canon.

This is, for Hegel, an unfortunate turn of events.

In the period in question the Church presents the aspect of a world of miracle; . . . natural existence has utterly lost its stability and certainty. . . . The Divine is not conceived . . . under conditions of universality as the law and nature of Spirit, but reveals itself in isolated and detached phenomena, in which the rational form of existence is utterly perverted.[16]

But Hegel makes it clear that it is only from "our" (i.e., the enlightened Hegelian) point of view that the irrationality of Robust Faith is so lamentable: the faithful participants of Christendom and feudalism experience "a state of satisfaction and enjoyment."[17]

For Hegel, Faith is always held accountable to the standard of absolute consciousness, that is, the model of transparent, conceptual knowledge. Robust Faith is irrational and superstitious, then, to the extent that this model for knowledge is tenable. Some have argued that it is not:

Hegel has a notion of conceptual thought as self-transparent which we find hard to share today. Much of contemporary philosophy has been concerned with showing how the clarity of our most explicit conceptual formulations reposes on a background of which we are not fully aware and which we can perhaps never exhaustively explore. Much that is implicit, for instance, in the very system of concepts or classifications that we use to formulate our clearest thought remains unstated and possible unstatable.[18]

To insist upon an element of opacity in knowledge, to relax the quest to rationalize religiously expressed mystery, is to view Faith in a new light. Faith no longer need appear as an insightful but naive precursor to absolute consciousness; it can become instead a repository of historical evidence through which to question the possibility of transparent knowledge. Robust Faith becomes not the undisciplined, soon-to-be-transcended attempt to realize *Geist* but a sign of the irreducible element of opacity in the world. On this reading, which is consonant with the claim that Robust Faith accentuates elements in the Faith of the *Phenomenology*, Faith can be seen to convey our dark sense of the unstated conceptual background necessary to any explicit thoughts. And the persistence of Faith-like expressions across epochs reinforces the judgment that a transparent knowing is a chimerical pursuit.

One can see now why Hegel's account of an enchanted world, an account that always focuses on the "progressive" insights of a mode of consciousness, is dominated by a discussion of the Church and its formal doctrines. Although Hegel agrees that many experienced a nature filled with divine signs, he dismisses this belief as "a credulity of the most absurd and childish character."[19] The "moments of truth" in Robust Faith, to the extent that they existed, were embodied in the Church, not in a view of nature as enchanted. This choice of emphasis in turn leads Hegel to see the self of Robust Faith as anything but robust: the self is either an overzealous producer of silliness or an unthinking slave to dogma. But if we peel away the view of Christendom and feudalism as necessary but deficient stages in the progress of absolute knowledge, we are opened up to the interpretation that the self with a lived experience of a miraculous nature text was an active, creative self—a self that allowed for ambiguous relations within its knowledge.

The Hegelian desire for unambiguous knowledge, its pursuit of a thoroughly intelligible nature, shares much with the Enlightenment pursuit of scientific certainty. Thus, there is a sense in which Hegel's very characterization of Robust Faith is already in Enlightenment terms. Yet Hegel, as we shall see later, provides a powerful critique of Enlightenment. Although ambiguity or mystery can in no way be construed as a moment of truth in Faith for Hegel, but is instead its defect, the subtlety of Hegel's analysis of Faith and Enlightenment itself provides considerations capable of converting the putative defect into an important insight.

The interpretation of Faith as robust, therefore, lies within Hegel's texts; it seems to be there in spite of his philosophical crusade for clarity.[20] Glimmerings of it are present in his critique of Enlight-

enment and in his qualified defense of Faith. I give a generous reading of Hegel's own account of Faith, one supplemented by an ideal-
type account of Robust Faith, for Hegel is too anxious to transcend/
preserve Faith into the higher rationality of a philosophy made possible by Enlightenment. To reject the view of history as the movement of increasing rationality is to be more open to the question of
Faith's tenability or truth.

The Self-Effacement of Robust Faith

I said earlier that Robust Faith is an inherently precarious mode of
consciousness, that the will to believe in resemblances coexists with
the suspicion that the truth of things may not be so comforting. The
potential for the disenchantment of nature, the drifting of God from
earth and of faith from God, was always present. Hans Blumenberg's
The Legitimacy of the Modern Age is useful for developing this
claim. He argues that theological attempts to sustain a robust religious faith paradoxically had the effect of further weakening faith
in God, that skepticism was in part religiously induced. Before I
turn to the Faith of the *Phenomenology* I will explore briefly this
argument, for it helps to explain the defensive stance of Faith.

The first sign of trouble for a robust faith in Christianity came
early, says Blumenberg, and took the form of the problem of evil.
If God is the good creator, then why did he create evil? If we are
God's beloved creatures, then why are we thrown into a hostile and
dangerous world? Gnosticism attempted to solve the problem by positing the existence of two gods, a benevolent creator and a demiurge
responsible for suffering, deception, and evil. But this solution was
at odds with a conception of God as one, omnipotent, omniscient,
and benevolent.

To retrieve the world as the creation from the negative role assigned to it
by the doctrine of its demiurgic origin, and to salvage the dignity of the
ancient cosmos for its role in the Christian system, was the central effort
all the way from Augustine to the height of Scholasticism.[21]

Augustine's efforts to install the hegemony of the unified and all-powerful God were definitive. He had to show that God was neither the author of evil nor one of two gods. Augustine vindicates God and repudiates the demiurge by making humanity responsible for evil. The source of evil is sin, sin that God allows in order that the human be a free, willing, and reasoning being. This formulation, however, can show that God is one, benevolent, omnipotent, and omniscient only if some sin can be identified that is great enough to absorb the wickedness of the demiurge. Augustine could find no actual and individual sin that could bear this weight, and this led him to posit "the uniquely great original guilt of mankind and . . . its mythical inheritance."[22]

The irony of Augustine's solution to Gnosticism is that the all-powerful, all-knowing Christian God now appears to have put himself in a bind. If he is so great, so powerful, why didn't he create a free human being without evil? If Augustine responds that human freedom logically entails the possibility of doing evil, one can ask why God is constrained by the structures of logic he himself has designed.

Blumenberg sees medieval nominalism as an attempt to escape the downward spiral of these questions. It emphasized the absoluteness and incomprehensibility of divine will. We humans simply cannot understand the reasons behind divine will, for the world is "the pure performance of reified omnipotence . . . a demonstration of the unlimited sovereignty of a will to which no questions can be addressed."[23] God is nominalistic: we can know the bare fact of his creation, but can know no more about him or about his mysterious, gratuitous creation.

The intent of medieval nominalism was to shore up God, to underscore his power, to preserve faith by making the individual awed by God even if one can no longer see him in nature. But although nominalism sought to bring humanity "to the point of inevitable resignation and thus of submission to faith . . . , the imminent dynamics of the situation led to the contrary result."[24] If God can create and act in ways not penetrable by puny human reason, then it was no longer reasonable to assume that the signs of divine will are legibly inscribed in nature. And if God no longer speaks to us in the everyday world and is largely incomprehensible, it becomes increasingly difficult to orient our lives toward him. Nominalism thereby contributed to the disenchantment of the world, damaging the naive, unreflective, and very powerful version of Faith.

In the face of this defeat, believers then sought to move the locus of God from this world to the next. God no longer resides in nature in a way intelligible to us, but escape from evil is still theologically available through an ecstatic devotion to the supernatural God and transcendent salvation. This is the Faith of Hegel's *Phenomenology*, one characterized by a flight from the material world.

This Faith no longer has the luxury of purely affirming itself—it must now expend much of its strength defending itself in the face of a competing worldview, the world as *factum*, that is, as something done or made, a contingent state of affairs. This secular response to disenchantment seeks "to construct whatever may be possible in this particular world in the way of security and self-realization 'even if there is no God.'"[25] The opacity of nature-in-itself suggests that, in a world of human need, nature be construed from the vantage point of human need and desire.

As God was pushed out of nature in order to preserve his omnipotence, nature became indifferent to humanity. In an indifferent world homesickness returned. One response to this existential uncertainty was the attempt to master and control a nature conceived as "matter." And only a nature conceived as neutral matter could be rendered predictable and resecured.

The more indifferent and ruthless nature seemed to be with respect to man, the less it could be a matter of indifference to him, and the more ruthlessly he had to materialize, for his mastering grasp, even what was pregiven to him as nature, that is, to make it "available" and to subordinate it to himself as the field of his existential prospects.[26]

Along with this instrumental relation to nature comes the enhancement of the stature of humanity, and with Descartes the self as knower comes to ground and certify the world. The human subject was "consolidated."

Under the enormous pressure of the demands made upon it by theology, the human subject begins to . . . take on a new overall condition, which possesses, in relation to ambushes set by the hidden absolute will, something like the elementary attribute of the atom, that it cannot be split up or altered.[27]

The disenchantment of the world entails a more self-assertive, self-realized, and self-conscious human subject.

The Faith of the Phenomenology

The self-centered and materialist counterworld to Faith described by Blumenberg coincides with Hegel's account of Faith's modern partner, Enlightenment. We have thus caught up to the Faith of the *Phenomenology*.

Hegel introduces Faith by saying that the feeling of alienation has worsened and crystallized. The old order of things is breaking apart. The self whose body and soul once mirrored the patterns of the stars has been supplanted by "an absolutely discrete unit" confronted by a "hard, unyielding reality, and here the world has the character of being something external, the negative of self-consciousness."[28] The self has come to a painful awareness of its individuality.

The faithful consciousness, longing for a wholeness and community absent from the emerging modern order, believes that corporeal beings can be united with their universal element, their spirituality, only in a transcendent world. Although this transcendent world cannot be experienced in the here and now, it can be conceived in thought. Faith, says Hegel, attempts to step "out of its actual world into pure consciousness, yet is itself generally still in the sphere of the actual world and its determinateness."[29] Faith's attempt to locate one's true life in a world beyond, a world accessible only in "pure consciousness," poses obvious conflicts for a being actually existing in the mundane. These conflicts manifest themselves in the form of knowing characteristic of Faith. Faith, "the disrupted consciousness," uses a simple mode of representation (*Vorstellung*); it thinks in picture-thoughts.

The highest form of knowing, the form toward which the *Phe-*

nomenology leads, is absolute knowledge, where thought coincides with being. The picture-thoughts of Faith stand in contrast to this standard of knowledge. Picture-thoughts are imprecise images; they represent their object—for example, God—but the edges of this object shade off into indefiniteness. Picture-thoughts function as "symbols which strain to render a higher content,"[30] as gestures that struggle to express the link between human and divine but that cannot attain the clarity of the Hegelian Notion. Faith senses a reality beyond it to which it is related in an unspecified but direct way. The authority of knowledge through picture-thoughts comes primarily from its immediacy. The objects of Faith, here God and the beyond, are in a form directly graspable by the believing consciousness, and the truth of these objects does not depend upon confirmation by sensory data. Empirical evidence can neither prove nor disprove picture-thoughts. Hegel points out, however, that "the immediacy . . . is due to the fact that its object is . . . pure thought."[31] Parables are good examples of the way picture-thoughts find verbal expression: they attempt to evoke the deep and abiding relation between historical events and timeless truths, but they do so in a veiled way, using analogy, symbol, metaphor, and an appeal to shared but inarticulate beliefs.

It is important to differentiate the epistemological images of picture-thoughts from the resemblances of Robust Faith. Both are modes of knowing that contrast to a rationalistic knowledge; both attempt to unify experience, to explain the human relation to things and God. But resemblances function to expose *inherent* connections between spirit and matter or between animate and inanimate being, where differences between types of being are understood as various themes within a single text. In picture-thoughts these differences have become definitive splits. Here the spiritual world and the material world are from the start distinct and nonoverlapping realms. The task set before humanity (a task picture-thoughts perform in an insufficient manner for Hegel) is to reconcile these two originally alien realms.

Moreover, picture-thoughts are human approximations lodged in perceptions or thoughts: their inadequacy, that is, lack of transparency, stems from the limitations of a finite understanding grappling with the infinite. Picture-thoughts privilege the self; resemblances inhere in the outside world. Resemblances and their signs originate from God: we receive them, and although they fade off into mystery and indefiniteness as we receive them, they are never themselves "inadequate." As divinely intended clues, they function perfectly well, are fully up to their task; they tell us exactly as much as we humans need to know, even though the content available to us is incomplete. Perhaps picture-thoughts can be understood as devitalized resemblances, similitudes stripped of their macrocosmic support. An order partly discernible gives way to a world whose structures are unsettlingly vague.

The Dialectic of Faith and Enlightenment

The discussion of Faith alone can proceed no further: "We have now to look more closely at the specific nature of that of which it is the 'other,' and we must consider it only in connection with this 'other.'"[32]

Enlightenment, like Faith, is a response to the dispersal of an enchanted world. It, too, is struggling to be at home in its world, to find a relation with the social and physical environment that is again comfortable, unified, and meaningful. Enlightenment responds to alienation not by focusing on the "true" world beyond but by retreating into the human self—what Enlightenment themes have in common is the centrality of human being. I will explore several of these themes: the critique of traditional, mystifying ideologies; the minimal earthly role available to the God of enlightened humanity; the focus on material reality and the rise of experimental science; utility; the faith in human rationality and will; and the conception of freedom as release from particularity.

Enlightenment culminates in the pursuit of absolute freedom, an attempt to unify experience by conceiving everything in the world as the secure and eminently knowable creation of consciousness. The supersensuous, social, and natural worlds are debunked, disassembled, and redefined in terms susceptible to human rationality and plastic to human will. While from Faith's point of view Enlightenment reduces the spiritual richness of the world to our mundane experience of it, Enlightenment sees itself as "the Spirit that calls to *every* consciousness: *be for yourselves* what you all are *in yourselves—reasonable*."[33]

To examine Enlightenment's emphasis on the self and on the internal space of reason and thought is to begin to understand Hegel's claim that Faith and Enlightenment belong in common to the element of "pure consciousness." Each represents a withdrawal from the confused, transitional, and often superficial understandings of the official, public world; each is led, by the search for a more authentic existence, to return to the innermost depths of consciousness.

Enlightenment, as "pure insight" or the simple faculty of self-certain reason, is

a restless process which attacks and pervades the passive essence of the "matter in hand" . . . [and] which eliminates everything objective that supposedly stands over against consciousness, and makes it into a being which has its origin in consciousness. . . . [T]hat is to say, only the self is really the object of the self, or the object only has truth so far as it has the form of the self.[34]

In Enlightenment the urge to strip away all illusion and mystery, to uncover truth through reason, finds its purest expression. Contemporary practices of deconstruction have roots in Enlightenment; this is true despite serious differences between Enlightenment critique and deconstructive technique—the most obvious is deconstruction's repudiation of the pursuit of a unified, rational replacement for the disassembled social and theoretical myths. But Enlightenment, in its early stage, devotes itself almost exclusively to the destruction of Faith, putting off its positive project until later. In this destructive effort it functions as a precursor of deconstruction, and, like its more recent progeny, it depends upon its adversary for its own energy and direction.

The existence of Faith, then, in what is commonly understood as an enlightened age of reason is more than a pathetic remnant of a former epoch where the natural world was invested with divine significance. The emergence of Enlightenment itself helps to maintain Faith as a subordinate opponent. Indeed, if Faith ever acquiesced completely, then Enlightenment would cease to exist as Enlightenment. Enlightenment as negative critique cannot exist without some content—for example, the affirmations and practices of Faith—to demystify. Enlightenment "only manifests its own peculiar activity in so far as it opposes itself to Faith."[35] Put another way, the defects of Enlightenment would become more visible if its adversary Faith disappeared. The same is true for Faith; Faith asserts itself in the face of the dominating force of Enlightenment. One consequence of this confrontation is that modern Faith must be defensive. Attempts to preserve its distinctive insights into the human condition meet with only sporadic success, yet modern Faith is the mode of religious expression best able to coexist with secular reason and modern science and technology.

For Hegel, there are both internal and external sources of this loss of confidence, this self-effacing stance of Faith. Hegel shows how Faith—of its own accord and through the logic of its thought—comes to confront limits in its own understandings. Faith, like all Hegelian modes of consciousness before absolute consciousness, is drawn to issues and conclusions that it is unable to incorporate into its way of life. This is one important impetus for the dialectical movement of history. But Faith is not alone in the modern age; alongside it has grown a way of life that poses an external challenge—Enlightenment. This internal realization of tensions and this external critique combine in the *Phenomenology*: Enlightenment criticizes Faith by counterposing the clear, reflective ideals of Enlightenment to the picture-thoughts of Faith, and this counterposing is at the same time a public articulation of weaknesses that already haunt Faith internally.

Two examples will illustrate this:

(1) Faith asserts the existence of an ever-present yet not wholly comprehensible unity of the supersensuous and sensuous. This unity is expressed in the Eucharist: absolute Being is presented in the tangible bread and wine. This unity is both symbolic and actual—the sacrament is a celebration of the identity of symbol and fact.

Picture-thoughts also have this characteristic, for knowledge does not make the dichotomous distinction between ideational representation and actual presence (the "for-us" and the "in-itself").

(2) Faith believes in the unity of human history and the atemporal order of the universe. History reflects not only the course of human events but also the rationality of the divine spirit. For example, Faith does not dissociate the life of a mortal, Jesus, from his divinity and the timelessness of his words.

In both cases, Enlightenment steadfastly charges that Faith has confused two logically distinct categories—the material and the spiritual—and demands a more precise theoretical articulation of their relation. Enlightenment problematizes the simple unities of Faith, and Faith cannot reply, for its affirmations, by definition, are not susceptible to the sort of justification Enlightenment demands. Enlightenment condemns Faith's stance as *irrational*.

The crux of Enlightenment's critique is that Faith results not in the reconciliation of matter and spirit (or of body and soul) but in a repudiation of the sensible world. For Enlightenment, Faith relies on a deliberate naiveté, a stubborn refusal to perceive evidence disruptive of its worldview.

Just as it sees Faith in general to be a tissue of superstitions, prejudices, and errors, so it further sees the consciousness of this content organized into a realm of error in which false insight, common to the mass of people, is immediate, naive, and unreflective.[36]

The price Faith must pay, then, for its "solution" to the homelessness felt by post-Robust consciousness, is the denial of the historicity of Jesus and the materiality of bread and the affirmation of only a vacuous and mysterious "spirituality." Faith's retreat to the world beyond is an expression of a pathetic inability to come to terms with human embodiment (and mortality) and to acknowledge a measure of human responsibility for personal, social, and political conditions.

Faith might respond to these Enlightenment charges in a variety of ways:

(1) It might offer a shrug of indifference, content to live out its

understandings in blissful ignorance of any narrowly theoretical critique Enlightenment may provide.

(2) It might attempt a deconstructive reply. It could refute the charge of unreflectiveness by showing how no position can achieve full clarity of expression. It could charge Enlightenment with an unreflectiveness about the falsifications and simplifications required to sustain *its* clear and precise views.

(3) It might argue that Enlightenment's critique is based on a fundamental misunderstanding of Faith. This is the defense of Faith that Hegel himself offers: "Enlightenment distorts all the moments of Faith, changing them into something different from what they are in it [Faith]."[37] In its frenzy to free society from the irrationalism of religion and tradition, says Hegel, Enlightenment misses the core of Faith: Faith sets aside the particularity of the individual in order to accentuate the ontological interpenetration of humans, things, and God.

To faith, its absolute Being, while it is possessed of *intrinsic being* for the believer, is also at the same time not like an alien thing which is just *found* in him, no one knowing how and whence it came. On the contrary, the faith of the believer consists just in his *finding* himself as *this* particular personal consciousness in the absolute Being and his obedience and service consist in producing, through his own *activity*, that Being as *his own* absolute Being.[38]

Enlightenment was right, says Hegel, to bring out the hidden element of sensuousness and historical contingency in Faith's beliefs and practices, but wrong to view those beliefs as nothing but the reification of historically produced norms and to interpret those rituals as nothing but the celebration of earthly goods. Enlightenment "regards the object of the believer's veneration as stone and wood, or else as something finite and anthropomorphic."[39] Faith may have only an uncanny hunch that the human condition involves a spirituality and that individuals are inherently bound up with a larger social, natural, and even universal whole, but Enlightenment mistakenly attributes the murky and sometimes tradition-bound character of Faith to the utter falsity of its insights. Enlightenment can do so because its own inability to realize its own aspirations through the vehicle of abstract reason has not yet become apparent to it.

Although Faith at one time or another has responded in each of these three ways, the overall tendency of its reply has been something else: Faith attempts to "rationalize" itself along the Enlightenment model of reason, but in so doing depreciates its own insights. The key questions here are these: Why does Faith respond in Enlightenment terms? How is it drawn into a game designed by and for Enlightenment? In order to understand the seduction of Faith, more needs to be said about the modus operandi of the Enlightenment critique of Faith.

It is not true that the perspectives of theoretical reason, embodiment, and history are simply absent from Faith and that Enlightenment arrogantly imposes its own standards upon Faith. Faith already contains these, but as implicit moments of its understandings and practices. What is absent in Faith is the conceptualization of these moments as discrete, dichotomous categories:

> For Enlightenment does not employ principles peculiar to itself in its attack on Faith, but principles which are implicit in Faith itself. Enlightenment merely presents Faith with its *own* thoughts which Faith unconsciously lets fall apart . . . it merely reminds Faith when one of its own modes is present to it, of the others which it also has, but which it always forgets when the other one is present.[40]

Enlightenment also reminds Faith that, at least for now, Faith must live and die in the world it attempts to repudiate. Enlightenment "upsets the . . . household of Faith by bringing into that household the tools and utensils of *this* world, a world which Spirit cannot deny is its own, because its consciousness likewise belongs to it."[41]

Through picture-thoughts, Faith posits large, diffuse categories, but these categories are not without their specificity. They do articulate religious insights into theory and situate them in history, although not in the way Enlightenment demands. The doctrine of the Trinity, for example, is, at the very least, a *theoretical* position, and it acknowledges the embodiment of Jesus. And the unity of the Trinity is realized only when a savior is born into history. Faith, in its doctrine of the Trinity, implicitly subscribes to the standards for which Enlightenment holds it responsible.

And counter to Enlightenment's accusation of the irrelevance of Faith for this world, the mode of understanding expressed in the Trinity can be fruitfully applied to this-world issues. The example I will explore here is Faith's view of nature. Faith does not deny that embodiment forces humans to use and transform nature. After all, the similitude Robust Faith saw between the aconite seed and the human eye was partly for the sake of improving human vision. But Faith also has insight into the way nature provides the condition of possibility for our sensory, emotional, and intellectual existence. This intimacy of internal and external nature is best expressed, according to Faith, through religious symbolism. These two sorts of understanding about nature—the "instrumental" and the "expressive"—are intermingled in Faith. An enchanted view of nature is the best example of this.

However, the very terms "instrumental" and "expressive" are not fully appropriate to a discussion of Faith, for it is a distinction best suited to Enlightenment sensibility. Faith resists the dichotomy between instrumental and expressive as well as the split between animate and inanimate being, and this resistance is both its weakness and its strength.

The strength ought to be obvious by now, though Hegel himself only saw it imperfectly: Faith gives us a glimpse into another world, a pre-Enlightenment world where, for example, the relation to nature did not result in the masterful attitude of modern science and technology. It also glimpses the way in which the Enlightenment project of freedom, rationality, and control underplays limitations inherent in its project.

Faith's resistance to dichotomies is weakness because it prevents Faith from achieving a clarity of expression that is essential to a high level of theoretical sophistication. It is also true that Faith's simple and harmonious holism makes it vulnerable to the charge that its insights are not "practical" enough.

These are the weaknesses to which Enlightenment makes appeals. Enlightenment charges that Faith's unities can hold together only if left unexamined, that once the elements of these unities are isolated and exposed to the light of critical reason, the "unities" are seen to be a hodgepodge of obscure insights and confused ideas, not coherent wholes. Because Hegel understands the way this weakness of Faith is tied to its strength, he is critical of Enlightenment's wholesale condemnation of Faith. Yet Hegel shares Enlightenment's visionary commitment to the precise concepts that result from a systematic, self-reflective epistemology. Enlightenment strives to make its philosophical categories as well as its social practices fully susceptible to rational analysis and pursues a theoretical articulation of those categories and practices that is clear, precise, and sophisticated enough to capture their complexities. Hegel calls this the pursuit of self-consciousness.

Although Enlightenment gives primacy to this pursuit, says Hegel, the potential for self-consciousness is given in all modes of consciousness. Faith "has within it the moment of reflection-into-self, or of self-consciousness, separated from its naivete, in the shape of an insight which remains independently in the background. . . ."[42] Thus, Hegel describes the Enlightenment critique of Faith as one whereby Enlightenment discloses to Faith the presence of its own latent, underdeveloped powers of self-consciousness. Enlightenment draws on this inner affinity of Faith for Enlightenment and exposes an aspect of the self of Faith of which Faith was only darkly aware. Faith is impressed by the disclosure as it recognizes itself in the critique; the legitimacy in Faith's own eyes of its picture-thought knowing is weakened.

One can see now why none of the above-mentioned responses to the Enlightenment critique is readily available to Faith. Faith's own capacities for theoretical reflection are aroused by Enlightenment, thus indifference toward Enlightenment's critique is impossible once Faith recognizes itself therein. For both Faith and Enlightenment subscribe to the criterion of articulation of knowledge. Moreover, Faith's self-consciousness is not yet developed enough for it to offer either the deconstructive or Hegelian replies.

Enlightenment charges Faith with a stubborn refusal to perceive evidence disruptive of its worldview. Now one can see why modern Faith is so stubborn. Its tenacity is a defensive technique. An enchanted view of the world is merely vestigial; it has to assert itself much harder. Faith, says Hegel, is properly insistent in some ways—it does see that Enlightenment's conceptual confidence stems from a systematic oversimplification of reality. Faith sees this flaw and itself acknowledges the complexity of reality even while it is unable to articulate this richer understanding.

The Hegemony of Enlightenment and the Persistence of Faith

But despite these moments of truth in Faith, Enlightenment establishes itself as the dominant mode of consciousness. Faith "has been expelled from its kingdom" and is a "yearning . . . which mourns over the loss of its spiritual world."[43] Faith, however, still "lurks in the background" to haunt Enlightenment. Insights of Faith endure, both in overtly religious positions and incorporated into Enlightenment itself. Faith is indeed infiltrated by Enlightenment categories, but Enlightenment also internalizes elements of Faith. "Enlightenment is caught up in the same . . . conflict that it formerly experienced in connection with faith," only now "it contains within itself the principle it is attacking."[44] Hegel's dialectic now focuses on the different modes of Enlightenment.

Enlightenment reappropriates moments of Faith, but this reappropriation, says Hegel, is often as much a transformation as it is a preservation. Faith's concern with a realm of nonhuman reality, with the enduring essence of Being, was focused around a specific divine person, God. Enlightenment follows Faith as it too attempts to conceive Being in theological terms. But the role of God in the enlightened world will be quite different from the role he would play in an era dominated by Faith.

Faith, through picture-thoughts, was able to integrate God and earthly existence. As long as this integration was unchallenged, the world included a reality irreducible to human intentions, creations, or by-products. But the Enlightenment's theoretical treatment of the concept "God" and its exposure of flaws inherent in Faith's picture-thoughts make it increasingly difficult for Enlightenment to consider the existence of any nonhuman being.

Hegel explains this claim through a discussion of Enlightenment deism and Enlightenment materialism. Through these two distinct but connected moves, Enlightenment internalizes Faith. Deism affirms the existence of absolute Being but insists upon purifying the notion of Being through philosophical analysis. The aim is to demystify the mysterious God of Faith. Deism seeks to transform Faith's loose picture-thoughts, to distill them, to have them congeal into clear concepts.

The essence of the concept "God," says the deist, is the otherness of his nature when compared to human nature—his supersensuousness, infinity, immortality. Hence there is practically nothing we can know or say about him, for any claim to knowledge or descriptive assertion would entail the attribution of perceptible, sensible, determinate (i.e., human) characteristics to him. No predicates can be assigned to God, hence knowledge of him is limited in the extreme: one can only know that he is, not how or why or in what way. (Deism is the heir of medieval nominalism, even though there are differences. The God of nominalism, for example, was conceived as an awesome, powerful being, whereas deism conceives a cool, efficient, but distant God.)

Deism does not deny Faith's God; rather, in its refusal to defile God with predicates, it sees itself as according God his proper respect.

To let nothing of that sort appertain to absolute Being . . . is the prudent behavior of Reason . . . which knows how to put itself and its finite riches in their proper place, and how to deal with the Absolute in a worthy manner.[45]

The result, however, of this respectful purification of God is his emasculation: "absolute Being becomes . . . a vacuum."[46] Hegel argues that a God about which one can know nothing in particular cannot loom large in consciousness or human affairs. Indeed, this God cannot continue to be understood as existing in any real sense.

Materialism, the other side of Enlightenment, takes the step from the epistemological skepticism of deism to atheism. It completes the deist demystification. Why hold on to the now merely formal profession of God's existence? Materialism denies the existence of God and a supersensuous or spiritual realm and turns its attention toward finite reality. Enlightenment now "isolates the actual world as . . . [sheer] determinateness [and] . . . unmoved finitude."[47]

For Hegel, materialism and deism suffer from the same defect. The ontologically privileged realm, whether that of absolute Being or matter, is conceived too abstractly. This charge of abstractness means that neither notion is intelligible, for neither can be embodied in words, theories, or practices. "Absolute Being" and "pure matter" by definition preclude any such embodiment:

It is important to bear in mind that *pure matter* is merely what is *left over* when we *abstract* from seeing, feeling, tasting, etc. . . . What is seen, felt, tasted is not *matter*, but colour, a stone, a salt, etc. Matter is rather a *pure abstraction*.[48]

Like deism's God, materialism's matter is non-sense.

Enlightenment has thus come to be

undiluted *platitude*, and the *confession* of platitude; because it consists in knowing nothing of absolute Being or, what amounts to the same thing, in knowing this quite flat truism . . . that it is only absolute Being; and, on the other hand, in knowing only what is finite and . . . thinking that this knowledge . . . is the highest knowledge attainable.[49]

Faith's struggle to experience the world as a mysterious unity of spirit and matter is taken up by deism and thereby doomed to abstraction. Materialism, blind to its own abstractness, temporarily resolves the struggle by rejecting all that is spiritual.

For Hegel it is not so much that deism is replaced by materialism as it is that they function together as a pair. The character of Enlightenment is not so neat as the discussion above, for the sake of clarity, tends to make it appear: materialism never succeeds completely in the negation of everything nonfinite; it is still oriented in some way toward absolute Being, even as it denies it. Every figure of consciousness is always in a struggle with competing modes. The relationships among Robust Faith, modern Faith, deism, materialism, and later utilitarianism and the pursuit of absolute freedom do not constitute a linear progression. Rather, the model is one of parry and thrust, of advance and retreat, of variable degrees and kinds of success in a fight for predominance. It is possible to discern a historical trend—Faith eventually loses sway to Enlightenment—yet elements generally understood as distinctive of Enlightenment are produced only against the backdrop of persistent non-Enlightenment modes.

Utility

The turn toward finite reality marks the final defeat of the enchanted link between self and world. A new conception of this relationship is now needed. What ought to be the human posture toward finite reality? Hegel next traces the conceptual steps that lead Enlightenment to the conclusion that it is appropriate for humans to relate to the world in terms of use value.

The atheism of materialism, wherein absolute Being is regarded as an empty abstraction, suggests that finite reality has the character of pure "being-in-itself." It is self-contained, independent of God, and determined by internal laws. But when the moment of Faith latent within Enlightenment, that is, deism, comes to the fore, finite reality appears in the context of God's creation. Then, it is seen as deficient, humble, and indebted to divine Being (even though divine Being is unspecifiable and treated nominalistically). In this latter case, finite reality takes on the character of "being-for-another."

But Enlightenment will find this analysis of the "for-another" dimension increasingly problematic. It assumes God as its point of reference; God is the other of the "for-another" of finite reality; God is that upon which all reality is dependent. Yet a point of reference, in order to orient temporal acts and beliefs, must have a fixedness, a solidity, and the capacity to be clearly identified by those in search of orientation. It becomes apparent that while the exalted but attributeless God has residual presence in the age of Enlightenment (enough to spark the initial consideration of the status of the material world), it did not have the power to be its reference point for much longer.

The God of a robust Faith was the center and ground of all experience: he was the still-fertile creator, the site of efficacious intentionality, the locus of subjectivity. But as Enlightenment unfolds the human self emerges as the only being eligible for the position of reference point. There is thus increasing pressure to view humans as subject, as having a deep, complex inner or mental life, a psychology, a reflective self-consciousness. The principle of utility is the accomplice to this shift in ontological emphasis; it is the formalization of the view that reality exists in reference to human subjects.

Enlightenment now answers the question about the status of the material world in this way: because the material world has a dual nature, containing both a moment of autonomy and a moment of heteronomy, "everything is thus as much something *in-itself* as it is *for-an-other*; in other words, everything is *useful*."[50] Finite matter is unique in that it is what it is only insofar as it is instrumental or for something else—namely, humans. Its essence *is* its usefulness; its end is to be a means. The material world can, "properly speaking, be taken just as one needs."[51]

Although Enlightenment has not yet realized it, says Hegel, the principle of utility gives man himself an ambiguous status. Overtly, the human appears as sovereign subject, as reference point. As "one who has come from the hand of God" (and now takes his place), "*everything* exists for his pleasure and delight and . . . he walks the earth as in a garden planted for him"[52] The plants and animals of the garden become objects docilely waiting to serve humans. But the principle of utility also carries with it the implicit view that humans are finite objects and can be used as such. Because of his embodiment, the human is also part of the material world.

But Enlightenment does not thematize the dual nature of humans as subject/object. Thus, it does not fully confront the problematic moral and political consequences of utilitarianism.

In reducing everything speculative to the human, it seems that the Enlightenment reaches a world of no depth, a world in which things are only what they are immediately, and a world in which individuals are . . . linked to each other only by considerations of interest.[53]

Enlightenment often covers up these consequences as soon as it raises the possibility of their discussion. Faith, the mode of consciousness still lurking in the background, periodically emerges to make the point about the underside of utilitarianism. And Hegel, in his analysis of Enlightenment's conception of freedom, dramatizes this underside.

For now Enlightenment can sidestep the issue only because it has a faith in reason and will. Although utility "can go beyond itself and destroy itself," says Enlightenment, this rarely occurs, for man is the "Thing that is *conscious*"[54] of the implications of utilitarianism. Man comes equipped with reflective powers—that is, reason— that can limit the overextension of utility. "Reason is for him a useful instrument for keeping this excess within bounds, or rather for preserving himself when he oversteps his limit." Reason is also called upon to ensure that utility will be channeled in socially beneficial ways: "Just as everything is useful to man, so man is useful too, and his vocation is to make himself a member of the group, of use for the common good."[55] Reason, for Enlightenment, is our God-given ability to discern, formulate, and adjudicate between moral principles; will is the invocation of reason.

The Enlightenment conception of reason exemplifies how the enchanted world of Faith persists. It persists as the continued adherence to a creationist ontology. God as designer of the universe is not dead. He designed the "garden" in which Enlightenment man feels free to manipulate objects, and he designed human subjects with a fail-safe device called reason.

There is certainly a way in which Enlightenment is full of hubris. Enlightenment glorifies the power of human reason and will, and it regards nature as matter in the service of human needs and desires. But the Enlightenment utilitarian is not a radical subjectivist. The useful object is still understood as an object with a moment of autonomy. "Utility," says Hegel, "is *still* a predicate of the object."[56] Enlightenment utilitarianism attempts to relate finite reality and human being by subordinating the former to the latter, but it does not completely subsume reality into subjective conscious-ness. The nonhuman thing continues to have an objectivity that stands opposed to self-consciousness.

Consider, for example, the deist claim that it is only with regard to things of sense that knowledge claims can be articulated or pred-icates assigned (thus God is indescribable). It implies what Hegel calls a sense certainty: "Consciousness . . . returns . . . to . . . a knowledge of what is *purely negative of itself,* or of things of sense, i.e., of things which *immediately* and indifferently confront its *being-for-self.*"[57] The materialist shares this epistemological view and thus shares the deist faith that God has created objects onto-logically independent enough to ground human knowledge. Other-wise, objects could not perform their role as sensory stimuli; that is, there would be nothing out there to shout to the senses.

But as Enlightenment unfolds, says Hegel, it moves away from sense certainty and, in a burst of willfulness, toward the view that "things" are constituted by the categories of reason. Enlightenment here "grasps in general every determinateness, i.e. all content and filling . . . as a *human entity* and (*mere*) *idea.*"[58] Enlightenment consciousness "lets nothings break loose to become a *free object* standing over against it."[59] The status of "things" shifts from that of "objects" to "notions" or mental representations of objects. Ob-jects-turned-notions are second-order beings, the products of the cat-egories that organized an identity for an originally chaotic cluster of elements. Enlightenment, in its most fully developed form, "seeks to abolish every kind of independence other than that of self-con-sciousness, whether it be the independence of what is actual, or of what possesses *intrinsic* being."[60] "Consciousness" is beginning a new phase: the pursuit of absolute freedom.

Absolute Freedom

How is the reduction of objects to notions freeing? It frees the self, at least temporarily, from the alienation of existence in an "exter-nal" world. Now "the world is for it simply its own will."[61] Enlight-enment, whose overall aim has been to secure the "unity of Thought with its Object," culminates in the "penetration of the Ego into and beyond other forms of being."[62] For Enlightenment, the cure for homesickness is "the harmonization of Being" because "for the . . . Ego . . . , that which is diverse from itself . . . presents an object of dread."[63] Freedom requires a mastery of the outside world through human ingenuity—one might even say, through force. Hegel calls it a "*challenging* [of] the external world to exhibit the same Reason which Subject possesses."[64]

This new project, the project most closely associated with the French Revolution, is to secure freedom through the removal of *all* impediments to the pure exercise of will. God has receded, objects have been unnerved—but the particularity of an act of will still stands in the way of the pure will and absolute freedom. We "must know what the Will is in itself. . . . The Will is Free only when it does not will anything alien, extrinsic, foreign to itself . . . , but wills itself alone—wills the Will."[65] This task requires that will be universalized, unlimited by the contingency and finitude of any individual will. This explains the appearance in history of something like Rousseau's general will.

For Hegel the talk of a general will exemplifies the Enlightenment process of subsuming reality into universal "notions." What it means for reality to become "notion" is that all particulars—for example, all individual persons or acts or desires or thoughts—are departicularized and absorbed into a general, abstract category of reason. Universalization of will requires harmonization of individual wills. This means that freedom requires the abolition of differentiating social roles and the suppression of individual self-interest—

all social groups or classes . . . into which the whole is articulated are abolished; the individual consciousness that belonged to any such sphere and willed and fulfilled itself in it, has put aside its limitation; its purpose is the general purpose, its language universal law, its work the universal work.[66]

Communitarianism is the order of the day, and with this comes, of course, the call for a renewed individualism. Hegel here identifies a debate between collectivism and individualism that continues today. We have inherited a theoretical and political world that "divides itself into extremes equally abstract, into a simple, inflexible, cold universality, and into the discrete, absolute hard rigidity and self-willed atomism of actual self-consciousness."[67]

Hegel concludes this discussion of Enlightenment with a critique of the pursuit of absolute freedom. Because any action whatsoever of an individual is by definition particular and nongeneral, it will be interpreted by advocates of absolute freedom as counter to the universal needs of humankind. Thus, any and every particular action is suspect. A political movement that seeks absolute freedom is and can only be negative, says Hegel, and it is no surprise that the French Revolution results in the terror of the guillotine, the denial of civil liberties, and indiscriminate acts of violence. Universal will can only act to destroy that which is established. When its advocates try to build or to express affirmatively the universal will, they find they can only issue in particular actions. For after all, any action is a particular action.

Before the universal can perform a deed it must concentrate itself into the One of individuality and put at the head an individual self-consciousness. . . . But thereby all other individuals are excluded . . . so that the deed would not be a deed of the *actual universal* self-consciousness.[68]

The revolutionaries of absolute freedom do not, however, acknowledge this contradiction in their position. They offer another explanation for the fact that, despite the revolution, social life still contains factions, strife, and differences of opinion regarding the general will. They locate responsibility in the secret wills of evil individuals seeking to undermine the community: counterrevolutionaries. Absolute freedom thus becomes absolute terror, and the leaders seek out and destroy suspect individuals.

Enlightenment has completed itself in disarray and decomposition, according to Hegel. On one side, its reduction of the world to utility threatens to convert the self into a means and to undercut its ideal of freedom; on the other side, its attempt to realize a pure will threatens to engulf the particular self in an abstract universal that can only act to deny and destroy, never to build and affirm. Although Enlightenment, despite its bravado, has not eradicated Faith, it has transformed it. And despite this transformation, Faith has shown how Enlightenment views of knowledge, nature, and freedom are problematic and often at odds with one another. Neither side has really won; there is an impasse.

NOTES

1. My account of an enchanted world is schematic. More developed philosophical readings can be found in Michel Foucault, *The Order of Things* (New York: 1970); Ernst Cassirer, *The Individual and the Cosmos in Renaissance Philosophy* (Philadelphia: University of Pennsylvania Press, 1963); Clarence J. Glacken, *Traces on the Rhodian Shore* (Berkeley: University of California Press, 1967); Hans Blumenberg, *The Legitimacy of the Modern Age* (Cambridge: MIT Press, 1983); Charles Taylor, "Rationality," in *Rationality and Relativism*, ed. Martin Hollis and Steven Lukes (Cambridge: MIT Press, 1982) and "Language and Human Nature," A. P. Plaunt Memorial Lecture, Carleton University, 1978; John Huizinga, *The Waning of the Middle Ages* (New York: Doubleday-Anchor, 1954).

2. Paracelsus, *Selected Writings*, ed. Jolande Jacobi (New York: Pantheon, 1958), p. 43.

3. Foucault, *The Order of Things*, p. 27. An interesting example of a faith in signs is Jean de Coras's 1561 analysis of the case of Martin Guerre, discussed in chapter 11 of Natalie Zemon Davis, *The Return of Martin Guerre* (Cambridge: Harvard University Press, 1983). The physical resemblances between the impostor Arnaud du Tihl and the real Martin Guerre disturbed Coras greatly. Could nature have deceived, sending false signs that allowed Tihl to pose as Guerre for several years? Coras concludes that the physical resemblances were not indicative of a truth of identity, but he does not also conclude that nature had allowed a false sign. God could not be so capricious. Coras resists an interpretation that undermines faith in the cosmos and offers instead one that keeps the prose of the world intact: Arnaud must be a magician, with a "dazzling power of deception. . . . Coras says he could not rid himself of this opinion even though du Tihl denied any diabolic art." (Davis, p. 109).

4. Foucault, p. 40.

5. Foucault, p. 35.

6. Glacken, *Traces on the Rhodian Shore*, p. 203.

7. Foucault, p. 34.

8. Foucault, p. 38.

9. Foucault, p. 31. Judith Brown's account of an investigation into the authenticity of a Renaissance mystic (*Immodest Acts* [New York: Oxford University Press, 1986]) provides an example of how the notion of microcosm helped to constitute what could be considered relevant evidence.

10. G. W. F. Hegel, *The Philosophy of History* (New York: Dover, 1956), p. 380.

11. Hegel, *The Philosophy of History*, p. 380.

12. Hegel, *The Philosophy of History*, p. 379.

13. Hegel, *The Philosophy of History*, pp. 389–90.

14. Hegel, *The Philosophy of History*, p. 390.

15. Hegel, *The Philosophy of History*, p. 390.

16. Hegel, *The Philosophy of History*, pp. 390–91.

17. Hegel, *The Philosophy of History*, p. 391.

18. Charles Taylor, *Hegel* (New York: Cambridge University Press, 1975), pp. 466–67. For another interesting critique of this aspect of Hegel see Joseph C. Flay, *Hegel's Quest for Certainty* (Albany: SUNY Press, 1984), especially the last chapter.

19. Hegel, *The Philosophy of History*, p. 413.

20. Taylor elaborates this point in *Hegel*, p. 539:

Now while Hegel's philosophy claims to be the fulfillment of Enlightenment thought, he in fact tries to combine with this, and with each other, two strands of thought and sensibility which were as much reactions to as extensions of the Enlightenment. . . . Hegel's philosophy can be seen as an attempt . . . to combine the rational self-legislating freedom of the Kantian subject with the expressive unity within man and with nature for which the age longed.

21. Blumenberg, *The Legitimacy of the Modern Age*, p. 130.

22. Blumenberg, p. 134.

23. Blumenberg, p. 171.

24. Blumenberg, p. 156.

25. Blumenberg, p. xix.

26. Blumenberg, p. 182.

27. Blumenberg, p. 196.

28. G. W. F. Hegel, *Phenomenology of Spirit*, trans. A. V. Miller (New York: Oxford University Press, 1977), par. 484. Reprinted by permission of the publisher.

29. Hegel, *Phenomenology*, par. 527.

30. Taylor, *Hegel*, p. 480. For another good account of picture-thoughts, see J. N. Findlay, *Hegel: A Re-examination* (New York: Oxford University Press, 1958), ch. 12.

31. Hegel, *Phenomenology*, par. 529.

32. Hegel, *Phenomenology*, par. 529.

33. Hegel, *Phenomenology*, par. 537.

34. Hegel, *Phenomenology*, par. 529.

35. Hegel, *Phenomenology*, par. 540.

36. Hegel, *Phenomenology*, par. 542.

37. Hegel, *Phenomenology*, par. 563.

38. Hegel, *Phenomenology*, par. 566.

39. Hegel, *Phenomenology*, par. 567.

40. Hegel, *Phenomenology*, par. 564.

41. Hegel, *Phenomenology*, par. 486.

42. Hegel, *Phenomenology*, par. 542.

43. Hegel, *Phenomenology*, par. 573.

44. Hegel, *Phenomenology*, par. 575.

45. Hegel, *Phenomenology*, par. 557.

46. Hegel, *Phenomenology*, par. 557.

47. Hegel, *Phenomenology*, par. 567. What "counts" for Enlightenment is finite reality. But what is the precise character of this turning toward finiteness? Is the claim that matter is all we can know? Or is matter all there is? Hegel suggests that it is both. All Hegelian modes of consciousness exhibit a conjoining of epistemology and ontology; the dialectical shift from one mode to another is a shift in both.

> The *Phenomenology* is a concrete history of consciousness, of its departure from the cave, and its ascent to science. . . . In the course of its development, consciousness loses not only what it held to be true from a theoretical point of view, but also its own view of life and of being, its intuition of the world. Experience bears not only on knowledge, in the narrow meaning of the word, but also on conceptions of existence.

(Jean Hyppolite, *Genesis and Structure of Hegel's* Phenomenology of Spirit [Evanston, Ill.: Northwestern University Press, 1974], p. 13.)

48. Hegel, *Phenomenology*, par. 577.

49. Hegel, *Phenomenology*, par. 562.

50. Hegel, *Phenomenology*, par. 560.

51. Hegel, *Phenomenology*, par. 559.

52. Hegel, *Phenomenology*, par. 560. See also Hegel, *Philosophy of History*, p. 440.

53. Hyppolite, *Genesis and Structure*, p. 440.

54. Hegel, *Phenomenology*, par. 560.

55. Hegel, *Phenomenology*, par. 560.

56. Hegel, *Phenomenology*, par. 582 (my emphasis).

57. Hegel, *Phenomenology*, par. 558.

58. Hegel, *Phenomenology*, par. 557.

59. Hegel, *Phenomenology*, par. 588.

60. Hegel, *Phenomenology*, par. 536.

61. Hegel, *Phenomenology*, par. 584.

62. Hegel, *Phenomenology*, par. 439.

63. Hegel, *Philosophy of History*, p. 439.

64. Hegel, *Philosophy of History*, p. 439 (my emphasis). The pursuit of absolute freedom is the logical result of Enlightenment. Its view of knowledge was immanent in the Enlightenment view that preceded it. The view

that knowledge is knowledge of perceptible objects shares something with the view that knowledge is knowledge of notions. Both endorse the primacy of epistemology, both presuppose that the most basic way of being in the world is knowing. And for both, "reality" is exhausted by what lends itself to clear representation—representation in human perception or human thought.

65. Hegel, *Philosophy of History*, p. 442.
66. Hegel, *Phenomenology*, par. 585.
67. Hegel, *Phenomenology*, par. 590.
68. Hegel, *Phenomenology*, par. 589.

Chapter 2

ENVIRONMENTAL MANAGEMENT
AND NATURAL HOLISM

HEGEL thought the dialectic of Faith and Enlightenment would come to a close as modernity was realized. But if the Hegelian solution to the dialectical impasse fails, and if Hegel's account is nevertheless powerful, one should expect to find manifestations of the impasse in the contemporary political world. Because advances in the power and destructiveness of science and technology are hallmarks of this world, the environmental debate is a likely site for the continuation of the struggle. This chapter explores environmentalism through the lens of Faith and Enlightenment.

Two Faces of Nature

Nature is both indispensable to human life and freedom and an impediment to them. It provides the material conditions for human survival even as it threatens the survival of some humans; it inspires human projects even as it precludes the realization of some conceivable projects.

Some seek to unify the two faces of nature by reshaping it into something less constraining and more responsive to human needs. They seek to transform a resistant nature into a hospitable environment, into docile matter standing in reserve for human projects.[1] But in acknowledgment of human dependence upon even an obedient nature, transformation must proceed, they say, in accord with a good resource-management plan. Let us call this orientation to nature, and the philosophical assumptions that support it, "environmental management."[2]

Others try to resolve the ambiguity of nature in the other direction. They argue that the impediments to human projects posed by nature need not evoke the managerial response once we ponder seriously nature's indispensability to human life and freedom. The relation between nature and humans is analogous, they say, to the relation between mother and child—we need only to convert our adolescent challenge to her as impediment to will into an appreciation of her as the providential boundary that allows will to assume a definitive shape. Let us call this orientation "natural holism."[3]

These different responses to the two faces of nature form the core of two environmentalist paradigms. Both wage war against social forms that were instituted before environmental consciousness had been raised. But within environmentalism itself wages another, internecine war between those who seek to perfect human mastery and those who seek a greater accommodation with nature.

It is a struggle in which hidden affinities between opponents create a debate that may obscure orientations to nature appreciated by neither party. For these disputants are, as Hegel leads one to suspect, also silent partners. They are partners, first, because each is formed through recognition of its opponent's defects, and second, because they share a similar premise about nature. This chapter uncovers the implicit views of nature, self, and freedom of each environmentalist paradigm, discovers a shared assumption inside their silent partnership, and introduces an orientation to nature that challenges the hegemony of the established debate. But I turn first to a fuller discussion of management and holism.

Environmental Management: Faith in Technique

The environmental manager repudiates the premodern faith that nature is designed to harmonize with human projects. So human needs, purposes, and aims must be imposed upon it. Nature, disenchanted, appears as a potentially troublesome, potentially useful field of electrical charges, chemical interactions, plant and animal biologies, mineral deposits, and so forth.

The environmental manager has faith, however, in human reason, science, and technology—in technique in its broadest sense as human contrivance. The environmental problem, once properly isolated, will find its solution in better planning, organization, and instrumental control; dangerous side effects of the project of control can be contained by new and improved techniques. The manager has a diverse array of contrivances at his disposal—mechanical devices, engineering plans, tax incentives, legal procedures, bureaucratic regulations, even philosophical arguments. "There is every reason to believe that technology could be harnessed, in as yet unknown ways, to diminish rather than to increase pollution,"[4] but even if "technology" fails, technique won't.

The manager deploys techniques to rationalize nature and to render it predictable, to replace its self-sustaining, "wild" state with well-managed industrial, commercial, residential, and recreational sites. And the assumption is that any clash between the natural order and the human redesign will ultimately be resolved in favor of the latter—for have we not already bred plants and animals to human specifications? The control of nature is one dimension of an Enlightenment quest to resecure a place for humans in a disenchanted world. The insistence upon control manifests itself also as an attempt to discipline the self by sublimating the nonrational, impulsive, or animal-like; as an attempt to order the social world by standardizing irregular beliefs, practices, or populations;[5] and as an attempt to rationalize the economic system by rooting out inefficiency.

The environmental debate has devoted a large share of attention to the last task. A rational economy is one where the social costs of production, including pollution, are factors in economic decisions. Until recently, environmentalists considered government regulation to be the best means to this end.[6] A public agency would determine how much of each pollutant could be safely discharged into the environment and to ensure that these "threshold values" were not exceeded. But environmental economists became increasingly critical of the regulatory approach—its demand that a bureaucracy establish, monitor, and enforce "safe" levels for each major pollutant was too ambitious; its legislative focus spawned litigious responses by corporate polluters; it was silent about recycling, internal changes in the production process, or production priorities; its interventionist logic was at odds with entrepreneurial freedom.

They responded to these flaws with a market-incentives approach. It would assign a price, in the form of a tax, to each unit of pollution. For if industry was forced to pay the social costs of its products—to internalize the externality of pollution—it would have a financial incentive to conserve resources or minimize environmental damage. The key, of course, is to set the tax higher than the cost of any pollution-reduction strategy a firm could devise.

Advocates of the pollution tax claimed it was more compatible with economic freedom than was government regulation, for each firm could choose its own method of pollution reduction. As an additional advantage, it relied only upon the self-interest of producers. It assumed no special civic virtue, only that producers seek to reduce costs and increase profits. Social behavior would be changed by modifying incentives that induce people to act rather than by mandating or prohibiting certain acts. One notes, however, that although the marketeers may be more successful than the regulators in preserving entrepreneurial discretion, their scheme too requires considerable government activity. Some public agency still must measure the output of pollution from each source in order to set a tax that approximates the marginal social cost of pollution.

A related attempt to force producers to internalize the social costs of production involves the concept of amenity rights. Although industry is now required to compensate property owners for damage resulting from pollution, the law does not yet require compensation for damage to peace and quiet, clean air or water, or privacy. If these amenities were given legal standing, there would be a financial incentive for industry to prevent damage by manufacturing quieter, cleaner, less intrusive products.

The different environmentalist approaches just described—the regulatory, the tax-incentive, the amenity rights—all assume that the environmental problem is susceptible to rational control. The nature problem is first defined as a problem of pollution and then assigned to the public policy specialists. Even though economic techniques must be supplemented by less reliable political ones— "The difficult questions now are not whether physical and economic problems can be solved, but which problems to solve and how to solve them"[7]—the faith in technique endures. The internal debates of environmental economists and policy scientists continue to center around which technique is best—regulatory, market-incentive, or legal-incentive? And all three strategies agree that none must seriously impede the individual's ability to consume or produce, for the good life is tied to continued increases in production and consumption, that is, to economic growth.

The faith in environmental technique recalls Enlightenment's faith in a self-monitoring, self-correcting reason. "Ignorance is one of the most potent obstacles to solving our ecological problems, an ignorance which only science can dispel."[8] Scientific reason operates at peak efficiency when the individual is not constrained by customs, traditions, conventional wisdom or superstition—when the unique, creative ingenuity of the policy or physical scientist is free to roam. (But this model of autonomous, reflective reasoning is at odds with the detailed, extensive, centralized regulation required by each environmental-management scheme.)

The goals of these strategies—efficient use and distribution of resources, the preservation of economic freedom, a high material standard of living—presuppose a view of nature as lifeless resources for use. Nature has the ontological status of matter for environmental management; this matter is sometimes seen as having a latent potential that can be realized only in collaboration with science and technology. Nature is a resource in need of technological fulfillment.

Half a century ago the air was for breathing and burning; now it is also a natural resource of the chemical industry. Two decades ago Vermont granite was only building and tombstone material; now it is a potential fuel.[9]

If nature is matter, then when we use it we are treating it in the manner appropriate to the type of being it has. No wrong is done when technique reorders nature; rather, it perfects it, it allows it to realize its essence. The use of nature by humans is mutually beneficial, not merely exploitive. Here we see how the manager endorses an Enlightenment understanding of finite reality—nature-as-matter is what it is only insofar as it is instrumental or for something else; its end is to be a means.

The environmental manager usually sees this natural matter as quite amenable to technological reorganization. The very success of modern techniques suggests that, in the long run, nature will be mastered.

Few components of the earth's crust, including farm land, are so specific as to defy economic replacement, or so resistant to technological advance as to be incapable of eventually yielding extractive products at constant or declining cost.[10]

Although some go so far as to claim that scarcity of natural resources may never occur (for it is already possible to "escape the quantitative constraints imposed by the character of the earth's crust"),[11] most managers see the constraints on technical control as more serious. There are limits, they say, to the shape nature can be forced to assume, and our duty to perfect nature requires that we acknowledge them.

To perfect nature is to humanise it, to make it more useful for men's purposes, more intelligible to their reason, more beautiful. . . . But like good artists, men should . . . respect their material.[12]

This combination of transformation, use, and respect results in a relation to nature of mastery, but a mastery that disciplines and enhances rather than enslaves and destroys. Nature needs to be liberated from itself. Like a tantrum-prone child, nature can be freed from its petulance through the imposition of external constraints. Nature realizes itself through our transformation of it, and we realize our highest potential through this process as well.

Man's great memorials—his science, his philosophy, his technology, his architecture, his countryside—are all . . . founded upon his attempt to understand and subdue nature.[13]

Not only are humans forced to subdue, transform, and use nature in order to survive and establish a stable society, it is their moral duty to do so, for "it is only they who can create."[14]

This last environmental approach has shifted emphasis from the efficient and prudent use of resources to the need to acknowledge natural limits, but it is still a version of environmental management. Its primary orientation to nature is utilitarian and anthropocentric; it seeks to rationalize and domesticate nature.

I would like now to consider in some detail an environmentalist strategy that is more self-conscious about its opposition to the management orientation, yet is also unable to transcend it. This discussion will help us to understand the depth of the appeal of the management orientation.

Trees Should Have Standing

The resource manager does not go far enough, according to Christopher Stone in *Should Trees Have Standing?*[15] Environmentalism must become a way of life, a public ethic, as well as a set of economic, bureaucratic, and scientific techniques. Environmentalism must not only manage nature cautiously and efficiently, it must contain our hubris with regard to nature. Stone seeks to accord natural objects independent standing by granting them legal rights. Natural objects with rights could press for damages for injury to themselves. And the threat of a lawsuit would force humans to take environmental protection more seriously and encourage us to treat nature as more than an environment standing in reserve. Plants, animals, and ecosystems, no longer mere property, become potential litigants worthy of respect. "Until the rightless thing receives its rights," says Stone, "we cannot see it as anything but a thing for the use of 'us'—those who are holding rights at the time."[16]

Stone's good intentions are undermined, however, by the logic of his project. In order to defend this claim, let us examine Stone's notion of rights.

Rights, neither natural nor universal, are "legal conventions acting in support of some status quo,"[17] "hypostatizations" that "always have a pragmatic quality to them."[18] This view departs from the liberal doctrine of inalienable human rights and from the religious understanding that value has a divine source. Stone can find no basis for grounding the rights of nature in something that transcends human decision and convention. But because Stone has to conventionalize rights in order to extend them to nature, these rights become inherently susceptible to reversal or revocation whenever other human conventions or interests outweigh the desire to preserve nature. The selves who grant the rights are free to take the gift away when they choose.

Why is it fitting today, according to Stone, to lift the status of natural objects from property to rights-bearing litigants? The protection of property requires an identifiable human owner who would be harmed by nonprotection. In cases of environmental harm, the owner is often difficult to identify. It may be, for example, the general public or the future inhabitants of a region. The extension of rights to natural objects would obviate the need to defend a diffuse or nonexistent owner. Thus, the rights of "unborn generations [or] . . . distantly injured contemporary humans"[19] would be better protected.

Like the bureaucratic and market strategies discussed earlier, the legal-rights approach seeks to incorporate into the legal system that which should be included by its own logic. "The river polluter's actions are costless, so far as he is concerned—except insofar as the legal system can somehow force him to internalize them."[20] Legal coercion requires that a monetary value be assigned to an environmental injury, and Stone suggests that these values be based upon the losses to industry requiring the unpolluted site or upon the cost of returning the degraded area to approximately its original state. It is often impossible to assign a dollar value to some environmental losses, but society is better off with rude estimates than with none at all.[21]

Stone is critical of a utilitarian orientation to nature, but his own position is too easily accommodated to it. For it is difficult to make sense of Stone's distinction between a natural object that is a "thing for the use of us" and a thing that has "received its rights from us." In both cases, human needs and aims are given primacy over the things and processes they define and govern.

Stone's anthropocentrism also surfaces in his consideration of how inanimate or mute objects could participate in legal proceedings. Suggesting that we handle this "as one does the problem of legal incompetents—human beings who have become vegetable," Stone recommends that a human guardian be designated by the court "to manage the incompetent's affairs."[22] Nature is here conceived on the model of deficient humanity.[23] Like the psychologically or mentally disabled, natural objects are judged according to an external ideal that they can never fully realize. They are thus deemed valuable to the extent that they resemble or can be made to resemble human litigants. This vision of nature as inferior humanity reflects and helps to constitute what much of nature has today become— the domesticated product of human technique.[24]

Stone's argument that "the strongest case can be made from the perspective of human advantage for conferring rights on the environment,"[25] admittedly employs a broad notion of what counts as advantageous to humans. To elevate the legal standing of nature through righthood not only can improve our material standard of living but, by enlarging our empathy and our sense of interdependency with nature, also can make us "far better humans."[26] Nevertheless, despite this broad notion of utility, and despite the distance he puts between himself and purely anthropocentric perspectives, Stone's approach presupposes a view of nature as value-dependent upon humans.

This is not to say that Stone believes that nature was designed to serve humans; in his view, there is no telos in nature. Rather, he implies that since nature has no discernible telos, there is nothing immoral about using it to our advantage. The resistance of nature means only that we must anticipate technical obstacles in order to overcome them in the future. Stone's defense of the rights of natural objects, his opposition to the view that natural objects are "for man to conquer and master and use,"[27] must be seen, then, as a species of utilitarianism; it is governed by the advantages it brings to the human user. No ontological violence is done to natural objects when they are conquered, mastered, or used; their rights are human conveniences—which may become inconvenient.

Stone explicitly endorses the distinction between the instrumental value of natural objects and their intrinsic value, and he seeks to create legal space for the latter. But he can sustain only a distinction between instrumental value narrowly construed (where natural objects are used indiscriminately and without regard for consequences) and enlightened instrumental value (where objects are used with awareness of the ecological, economic, or recreational needs of living humans or their descendants).[28] He accepts, therefore, the natural ontology of environmental management while modifying slightly the policy priorities it typically advances.

This bias in favor of nature as useful matter is implicit in Stone's ambiguous articulation of his project. He seeks the "independent standing" of natural "objects," but this standing is a function of rights "granted" by humans. To talk of the standing of natural objects is to presuppose already the centrality of humans. A subject always determines the value of an object; an object is that which can only be constituted by a subject for whom it exists. And value cannot be intrinsic or independent if it can be bestowed by an outside entity. The very distinction between instrumental and intrinsic value is faulty in the context of a discussion of nature conceived as object.

Robin Attfield, another environmental ethicist, also sets out to defend the "intrinsic value" of nature, that is, value that exists "independently of any awareness . . . on the part of any conscious being."[29] "Any theory of value," he says, "however instrumentalist in tenor, must recognize intrinsic value somewhere, or there is nothing which gives anything of value its point."[30] But Attfield does not succeed either, for this defense of the intrinsic value of nature is just as much a defense of the view that human subjectivity is the genesis of value—that human aims, needs, or ideals give value "its point."

Stone's notion of independent standing, like Attfield's intrinsic value, is a category mistake. It is analogous to an "accidental intention"—each term is inimical to the other it is supposed to qualify. And the conceptual incompatibility expresses a deeper tension in Stone's theory, that between the desire to respect nature on its own terms and the need to impose human form upon a nature no longer predisposed to humanity.

It is this latter need that carries the most weight for Stone and most of the participants in the environmental debate, and it is what leads them to view nature as useful matter. But why does it carry so much weight? What are the pressures at work that draw even those who resist toward a view of nature as standing reserve?

The Appeal of Management

An underground source of the appeal of environmental management is the desire to see oneself as free, where freedom is understood as the enlightened expression of an individual will. Thus, the view of nature as dead, meaningless matter is so powerful because it appears as the prerequisite to a view of self as alive, purposive, psychologically deep, and capable of autonomy. In short, nature as standing reserve is part of the managers' attempt to see themselves as potentially free subjects—for how could humans be free subjects if nature was not objective, devoid of meaning and intrinsic value?

The manager fears that to question the view that humans assign value to meaningless matter is to come too close to the view that human worth depends upon its biological contribution to nature; to deny that nature is properly defined by its utility is to court the medieval view that nature has a subjectivity and a teleology; to argue that nature is more than a means is to risk saying that it is an end in itself; to criticize the rational, scientific investigation of nature is to advocate an irrational, primitive, or mystical orientation.

Environmental management is careful to distinguish, in theory and in practice, among nature (that which is given), society (that which is a human creation), and humanity (that which wills and creates). These distinctions are part of the painstaking process of civilization, of the rescue of humans from submersion in the realm of necessity. *We* are increasingly self-determining beings; *nature* is a background environment that, although not static, does not move in any obviously teleological way. Nature is not designed for us or by us, and

only if men see themselves . . . for what they are, quite alone with no one to help them except their fellow-men, products of natural processes . . . wholly indifferent to their survival, will they face their ecological problems in their full implications.[31]

According to environmental management, the only way around an instrumental view of nature is to deny at some level the disenchantment of the world. Natural holists, for example, do not see humans "for what they are," because they cannot bear to accept the disappearance of telos from nature. Instead, they still seek in nature principles that could guide an ethical or social order and signs that could reveal the human essence or meaning of life. While this quest for meaning is an enchanting idea, compatible with a world of Robust Faith, it is radically incongruent with modern institutions, sciences, roles, and norms. Holistic orientations to nature, because they exaggerate the enabling face of nature, always have a hollow ring. They routinely become abstract and vague visions, not lived orientations to nature.

Let us place environmental management's self-justification in the context of the dialectic of Faith and Enlightenment. Like Enlightenment, environmental management has defined the alternative in stark oppositional terms. It has contrasted itself to an implausible alternative presented as the only alternative. And once this implicit move is accepted, the case against the alternative is already made; its dichotomous understanding loads the dice in favor of nature as standing reserve. Environmental management defines its opponent in terms that are incredible to modern discourse, thereby ensuring its own hegemony within the established terms of debate.

Controlling the definition of what counts as a rational theory of nature, for example, it is able to relegate utterances based upon other definitions to the realm of irrationality and superstition. In endorsing the modern dream of a clean, odorless, and glamorous life, it can define a life lived in close contact with nature as primitive. In tune with a science that aims to render transparent the mechanisms of nature, it classifies knowledge that finds opacity in nature as mystical. An extreme version of environmental management even fears that contact with "raw" nature may result in a "highly strained imagination . . . the source of fanatical religious and superstitious terrors."[32]

I will argue later in the text that natural holism also defines its opponent narrowly through a simple contrast to its own favorably interpreted views. It does attempt, however, to avoid this dichotomous thinking in its internal understandings. It struggles, for example, to resist either/or categories in order to embrace an organic model of knowledge reminiscent of picture-thoughts.

Environmental management places its opponent within a frame that makes it easy to dismiss, yet it never actually dispenses with it. Quite to the contrary, it continually revivifies what by its own account ought to be a decaying and anachronistic body. It does this because, like the parasite that saves the vital organs of its host in order to prolong its feast, it requires its opponent, just as Enlightenment requires Faith.

Environmental management requires natural holism as content for its rationalizing critique; it needs messy raw material in need of clarification. It also requires it because the credibility of its own affirmations depends upon the audience accepting the management construal of the alternative position. For without this acceptance, the defects within environmental management would become more apparent, weakening its own hegemony. Environmental management has an ambivalent stance of rejection and engagement with noninstrumental orientations to nature. It claims to fear them as confused and regressive, but the exaggerated characterization of their confusion and regressive potential suggests that what is really feared is the disappearance of such views. Environmental management darkly recognizes its dependence on them as a foil for its own weaknesses.

Nature and Order

The preceding discussion has tried to show some of the ways Enlightenment modes of thinking have found expression in the environmental debate. It has also suggested that the appeal of the managerial orientation stems in part from its power to set the terms of debate, to determine the set of possible alternatives. Finally, it has contended that, like Enlightenment's dependence upon Faith, environmental management's critique of the holist view is central to its own self-definition.

But what is the affirmative side of this critique? Clearly, management rejects the view that the order of nature harmonizes with human aspirations, but what kind of order can be ascribed to nature from within the managerial perspective? One can discern at least three different responses:

(1) *Nature as Nemesis.* One view of the order of nature consistent with management principles is that nature is chaotic, wild, and dangerous. The imperatives of human existence require mastery and transformation of nature. Far from being in harmony with human ideals, nature threatens them. This view is an integral part of the appeal and self-justification of environmental management.

(2) *Nature as Plastic.* Nature is benign and neutral. It is a messy conglomerate of functions, forms, and processes that require human ideals and projects to organize them. This assumption of plasticity finds expression in the view that nature is in need of technological fulfillment.

(3) *Nature as Indifferent.* Here the manager sees nature as neither an enemy nor a plaything; it is merely indifferent to human projects. It is ordered according to priorities not necessarily compatible with human rationality, psychology, sensibility, or perception. Because of this indifference it is likely that nature will appear as recalcitrant material. The assumption of an indifferent order is operative when management repudiates all residues of faith in a designed world, including the faith that nature requires humans to perfect it. Because faith in the accord of nature and humans is untenable, mastery is a justifiable response to nature.

The technological implication of all three views is, however, essentially the same: whether nature is chaotic and dangerous, benign and malleable, or indifferent and recalcitrant, the project of mastery is justified, as long as it avoids actions harmful to long-term human interests. Natural holism is an orientation to nature that rejects this common conclusion. For the holist, nature is not a deposit of resources, but a partner in the mutually engendering web of human and nonhuman life; science should explore nature not to conquer it but to find ways to accommodate human projects to it; there is no need to rationalize nature, for it already possesses its own rationality, and its beautifully complex design is already worthy of respect.

But is this holist view truly at odds with the scientific approach endorsed by environmental management? Has not modern science already incorporated elements of holism? And if so, isn't my distinction between environmental management and natural holism overdrawn?

Indeed, the categories of environmental management and natural holism are, like the categories Faith and Enlightenment, ideal types or representative modes of thinking. And there are several sites of intersection between management and holism. As a preliminary to my discussion of natural holism viewed from the inside, I will briefly explore some ways in which holism has permeated modern science.

Holistic Management?

Although the heterogeneity of "modern science" makes dangerous its use as a subject of a sentence, one can say that modern science assumes the existence of regularities in nature that can be predicted and controlled in the service of human aims. And its description, prediction, and manipulation of natural regularities has, in some impressive ways, paid off.

But although science assumes that nature has discernible regularities, it also concludes that nature contains inexplicable irregularities. Do not be surprised, then, if the pay-off is sometimes less than anticipated. Evolutionary theory, for example, argues that within nature a general tendency toward adaptation for survival coexists with evolutionary dead ends, maladaptations, and mistakes. And according to quantum theory, nature is a field of chance rather than a composite of stable, rationally ordered substances.

One could conclude that science repudiates the holist belief in a harmonious fit between plants and animals or between human needs and the natural provision for them, that there is a significant difference between scientific claims about recurring natural patterns with some degree of internal coherence and the teleological claim of natural holism. According to this line of reasoning, evolutionary theory cannot be seen as evidence of telos in nature; the theory is incompatible with the holist dream of "universal kinship and common bonds of function, experience and value among organisms."[33] Evolution does not imply the kind of telos where the world is a purposive order, nor does it even guarantee that the world tends toward a state of harmonious equilibrium. In other words, evolutionary theory does not provide the existential comfort that holists seek.

Neither does theoretical physics offer this comfort, one could continue. Rather, it leads physicists away from the view that the structure of nature coheres with the structure of human rationality. The implication of quantum theory is that because material particles of very small dimensions do not behave in ways that are theoretically determinate, there may be an insurmountable barrier between conceptualization and natural reality.

But although it is reasonable to argue that modern science is at odds with a natural holist view, there is also a case to be made for the opposite claim. From another perspective, the irregularities in nature, the dead ends of evolution, and the indeterminacy of subatomic particles can be seen as evidence that modern science endorses dimensions of natural holism. These discoveries could be interpreted as a scientific admission of the incompleteness of scientific knowledge and of the irreducible element of mystery within scientific theory. The regularities of evolutionary development can be seen as signs of a designed universe and the irregularities of evolutionary development as signs of the discrepancy between finite human understanding and divine rationality. Environmental management takes for granted a model of certain and complete knowledge, but here science itself is led to an epistemology of indeterminacy, incompleteness, and mystery. There is a convergence between the scientific epistemology that management relies upon and the epistemology that holism explicitly endorses.

From this same perspective, ecology appears as another instance of the convergence of managerial and holistic orientations to nature. The ecologist, like the natural holist, calls into question the assumption that a particular natural element can be isolated and manipulated without serious consequence to other elements not means to the end at hand. The ecologist rejects this atomism in favor of a view of nature as a system of interconnected parts, an organic whole, and seeks to uncover functional interdependencies of members of an ecosystem. "The idea of the ecosystem . . . means . . . that a whole is greater than the sum of its parts, that a molecule of water is 'more than' the simple addition of hydrogen and oxygen."[34]

But the ecological perspective can also be distinguished from natural holism.

First, while ecology assumes that nature is a system of functionally interdependent parts, it resists the view that humans are simply another one of those parts—it cannot, from the perspective of a natural holist, shake the anthropocentric hubris. The ecologist finds it difficult to acknowledge the interdependency of all living and nonliving things without immediately following it with a disclaimer distancing humans from the web of interdependency: the uniqueness of a human "lies . . . in the special character of his relations with other systems . . . [i.e., his ability] to transform them."[35] The special status of humanity and the uniqueness of each individual require the rejection of the view of nature as a metaphysical whole wherein all differences are differences in degree.

Second, when ecology says that the natural whole is more than the sum of its parts, the "more than" does not include dimensions of life empirically unavailable. While holistic when compared to chemistry or the traditional biology of classification and dissection, ecology is still tied, if more ambivalently, to the dominant scientific paradigm. Nature is an ecosystem filled with complex and interconnected parts, but the parts are essentially physical and mechanical. "Kinship" among parts is survival-functional; it is the kinship of a shared evolutionary history or of a shared need for food, shelter, and air. Ecology is most comfortable when the world it engages is the world of matter. A central project of natural holism, on the other hand, is to articulate the threads that link material reality with dimensions of existence inadequately described as material.

Third, the explanatory power of ecology dwindles as one approaches less "natural" environments like suburban neighborhoods, city blocks, or industrial parks. Ecology can best describe the relationship between humans and nature when humans account for only a small percentage of the biotic community under study. This limitation stems from a theory that conceives the self primarily as manipulator of nature, rather than something itself shaped by internal and external nature. Thus, while ecology is alert to the ways humans disrupt nature, it is unable to elucidate how nature enables human actions. What are the implications of human embodiment for an orientation to nature? What is the connection between the structure of human perception and the natural world? How are humans a part of nature despite the fact that they are beings not exhausted by their physical form? These questions, important to environmentalists working within a natural holist frame, are beyond the ken of ecological science.

Nevertheless, ecological theory, as well as evolutionary and quantum theory, is an instance where an enlightened science draws near to the faithful approach of natural holism. There do seem to be points of contact between the managerial and the holistic orientations to nature, even though these scientific theories can also challenge religious interpretations of nature and even though systems theory can be distinguished from a harmonious holism. This incomplete convergence ought not to surprise, for to say that the Faith-Enlightenment dynamic manifests itself in the environmental debate is to affirm the mutually engendering nature of the partners in debate. Elements of each migrate into the other and mingle with elements initially foreign to them. Thus, natural holism harbors, as we shall see, a secret respect for the precise method of science, and environmental management finds itself unable to ignore the ethical dilemmas within modern science.

Management and holism, as modes of Enlightenment and Faith, continually draw near only to diverge once again. They draw near because each bumps into its own limits as it pursues its project. They diverge as they respond to these limits differently and give different weight to similar considerations; each is governed by a different project it thinks susceptible to fulfillment. The Enlightenment project is the precise articulation of useful knowledge about nature; the Faith project is to show how nature cannot be captured in precise, utilitarian terms. Thus, the "same" phenomena—for example, the social costs of pollution or the rights of trees—are weighted differently by environmental managers and by natural holists. For the former, they are externalities, mere side effects of a morally neutral project of controlling nature; for the latter, they are flaws endemic to the very attempt to manage nature. For if one believes that there is an organic connection between the natural, moral, and social worlds, pollution and a lack of respect for nature are not contingent externalities but necessary and primary concerns.

The natural holist charges the environmental manager with a naive faith in science: no amount of technique can reverse our environmentally destructive path. An orientation to nature in terms of use value, despite any attempt to mitigate the most dangerous or distasteful side effects, must result in environmental affront. Moreover, such an approach to nature has pernicious moral consequences. A utilitarian orientation to nature helps to legitimate an instrumental orientation to humans. For natural holism, the tyranny of instrumental rationality, an often lamented hallmark of modern life, must be fought at the level of our orientation to nature if it is to be fought at all.

Natural Holism: To Experience Is to Believe

I turn next to two representatives of natural holism, Erazim Kohak and John Compton. What distinguishes their positions from the dominant managerial approach is a focus on experiential contact with nature. Such direct contact is, they claim, the best argument in favor of a view of nature as a harmonious whole. For Kohak, the nature to be experienced is the great outdoors, where a simple life in pursuit of basic needs will uncover the moral order of nature. For Compton, the relevant natural site is the human body, where an investigation of the structure of perception and cognition will un-cover the primordial belongingness of embodied selves to the natural world.

Natural holism, I will argue, conceives nature in terms reminis-cent of Faith. But the locus of faith has changed—the site of evi-dence that nature and self are in ontological accord is different. Robust Faith sought this evidence in an enchanted natural world; it stood in awe of the light of nature and the darkness of human knowledge. The Faith facing the eighteenth-century Enlightenment looked to the supersensuous realm; it sought to thematize spiri-tuality in an age of matter and to endorse picture-thoughts in an age of pretensions to scientific precision. Contemporary Faith, I ar-gue, now invests its hopes for signs of harmony in "lived experi-ence"—in the direct experience of nature in the wild or in a phenomenological understanding of the human body.

The Moral Order of Nature

Kohak understands the appeal of the managerial view of nature—it is inscribed in dominant ideals of self and freedom and thus pos-sesses the great political advantage of a view continually reinforced through everyday life. But Kohak defends a different set of views about nature, self, and freedom, arguing that the management set combines incompatible elements. A utilitarian orientation to na-ture inevitably fosters the treatment of humans as mere means, for embodied humans too can be seen as "natural objects." And to treat humans as objects—through genetic and social engineering, through marketing and manipulation of public opinion, through bureaucratic regulation of clients—is to undermine the view of the self as a responsible, self-determining, and free agent.[36]

When the manager does discern this incompatibility, he or she is likely to be drawn to an ethic of rights for natural objects, for this amendment requires no fundamental rethinking of management presuppositions. Yet the rights approach affords respect to that which is nonhuman, says Kohak, only to the degree that it approaches the standard of human subjectivity. It cannot shake loose its self-destructive anthropocentrism.

Environmental management fails to generate respect for external and human nature precisely because its outlook is secular, he continues.

> If there is no God, then nature is not a creation, lovingly crafted and endowed with purpose and value. . . . It can only be a cosmic accident, dead matter contingently propelled by blind force. . . . If God were dead, so would nature be.[37]

If God is dead, then nature was not designed for us. If we are thus always living dangerously, then the masterful reorganization of nature is our only rational response. In the absence of a created, purposeful nature, there can be no ethical orientation to nature. But have no fear, says Kohak, God does exist, nature does have a moral order, and we are capable of recognizing it. Here the holist's reasoning mirrors the manager's: the horror of the alternative is presented as justification of the original position. Holism, like management, requires its nemesis, once that nemesis has been properly characterized.

Kohak does not concede the death of God and then attempt to secure a secular ethic of respect for nature. Instead, he contends that a respectful orientation to nature, based initially on faith, will itself evoke the experience of God. A secular environmental ethic might respect nature for its sheer difference, its impressive resistance to human projects. But Kohak sees no distinction between intrinsic purpose in nature and a recalcitrant integrity worthy of human respect.

Natural holism has a faith that nature and self are in existential accord. Kohak's faith is religious: God is the guarantor of the harmonious potential of his creation. But the faith of natural holism can have different loci; it can lie, for example, in the cosmos, human nature, good will, rationality, the Tao, or Gaia. Kohak serves as a representative of natural holism because of the thorough and consistent character of his theory. He elaborates, I contend, teleological assumptions about nature secreted within a variety of orientations that counsel us to enter into a closer attunement with nature.

Respect for nature, according to Kohak, must be grounded in a recognition of the "eidetic structure of being."[38] Human minds and bodies are integral to this structure: "Though distinct in my own way, I yet belong, deeply, within the harmony of nature."[39] This harmony is evident to us as we note the craftsmanship of the beaver's dam, the helpful predictability of the movement of the stars, and the relaxing vistas of green landscape. Kohak's beautiful descriptions of nature, with their generous use of harmony metaphors, calm and seduce with the promise of a nonalienated relationship to nature. And after this longing to be at home in the world has been aroused, he encourages us to recall times in the woods or at the sea when we have "understood" (and not merely "explained") our world. He then makes the claim for which we have been prepared— our longing to be at home in the world can be fulfilled, if we allow ourselves to experience nature in an authentic way. Because all understanding "is fundamentally . . . the empathetic grasp on the intrinsic . . . rhyme and reason of its object,"[40] the human ability to "understand" nature implies the existence of a moral order within it.

But if the harmony of nature and humans is a primordial given, then why do so few people recognize it? We often fail to hear the eloquence of the cosmos, says Kohak, because we can no longer experience nature-in-itself. We have buried nature under a thick layer of abstract theories and explanatory models. Modern science, for example, mediates and distorts our relation to nature, substituting "a theoretical nature-construct for the nature of lived experience."[41] This substitution has its place—it is appropriate when we are "dispatching rockets to the moon"[42]—but it is powerless to address the moral dimensions of human and natural life.

But our inability to recognize that we belong to nature is not merely a problem of perspective. The moral order of nature would remain obscure even if we eschewed a theoretical approach to nature for a lived, experiential approach, because the nature with which we can be in direct, unmediated contact has already been, to a large extent, physically transformed to fit the theoretical model of science. Much of the outdoors has become artifact: fenced and regulated parks, perpetually noisy and glaring streets. We still have "lived experience," but the nature we experience is rarely that of nature-in-itself. Night has become a neon glow; food, a precooked and packaged meal. "Our estrangement from nature is no longer conceptual only: it has acquired an experiential grounding."[43]

But what, then, is the way to nature-in-itself? How do we approach that which presents itself not as our own making but as something "to be acknowledged, making its own demands"?[44] The enabling method, Kohak tells us, is to live for periods of time in "radical brackets," that is, apart from characteristically modern thoughts, institutions, practices, and devices. "We need to suspend, for the moment, the presumption of the ontological significance of our constructs, including our concept of nature as 'material,' "[45] and we must uproot our bodies from the artifact world and replant them in nature—for only the solitary immersion in nature undominated by humans will allow the moral order of nature to present itself to us.

The moral order will remain absent as long as we insist that humans are the only "presenters" and nature only a passive recipient. But this narcissism can be dissolved by the roar of the ocean or the stillness of the forest. There,

nature presses in. It is too vast for the human to outshout it, too close for him to withdraw from it into speculation. . . . [There we learn that] a human cannot impose . . . upon the world quite so easily.[46]

The solidity of the moral order of nature means that it does not bend to every and any will. Nature has its own way, its own integrity—it was designed. It is true that we have a place within this beneficent order of nature, that we belong, but we belong to it as well as in it. In short, we are not in control. The desire for control is indeed persistent, but it will dissipate once we acknowledge that nature is always already there—it stands before us waiting to be experienced, but it exists prior to experience.

Beneficent but not our creation, nature bestows gifts upon us. First, the gift of the night: "Were there no darkness to restore the soul, humans would quickly burn out their finite store of dreams. Unrested, unreconciled, they would grow brittle."[47] Night soothes ontologically as well as psychologically; it makes us whole, enabling the full range of human experiences, providing a setting where modes of being unexpressed during the busy day can come to the fore. One of these latent modes is an encompassing and easy wonder. When the first star makes its appearance seemingly from nowhere, for example, the awe that we experience does not require effort or even assent.

The . . . moon does not "shine." . . . All our words for lighting . . . are active verbs suggesting doing, while the moon does not do. It lets itself be seen, not crowding out the darkness but rendering it visible.[48]

At night, we can "be" like the moon. The darkness and inexactitude of the night relieve us of the pressure of doing, doing, and more doing, of explaining and interpreting and reenacting in our minds the mechanism of phenomena around us. The inescapable difficulty of working in the dark excuses us from the duty to do so; electric lights deprive us of the solace of darkness even as they illuminate.

How ironic, says Kohak, that nature soothes while the artifact world, our own creation, alienates.

The dominant colors of a forest . . . are green and light blue, both of which, as empirical psychology can attest, have a distinctly soothing effect. . . . The decibel levels here are geared to the tolerances of the human nervous system. . . . The environing world of a forest . . . is calm and unjarring, living its own familiar life, so unlike the threatening, unpredictable environment of the artifact world.[49]

Our senses are another gift of nature; they are dependent upon the world's cooperation with them. Sight is possible only because light, shadow, and form allow it. We can loosen our attachment to sight, sometimes even gratefully, in the vague and mellow world of the night. And then the gift of hearing can come to the fore, for experience is enriched as we simply listen, open to the voice of nature.

A third natural gift is the word. We often, of course, decline to accept the gift of language as it was intended. Nature is meaningless in itself, we say, and has only the use value of an artifact; thus, through language a society assigns and designates meaning to intrinsically meaningless material. This intersubjective version of solipsism is persuasive, says Kohak, only because it is repeated so frequently. But repetition loses its power to convince when we live in radical brackets. Then we see that meaning is not the product of individual will or collective convention but something that makes itself manifest in patient observation.

Kohak contends that actual experience of untamed nature will allow us to have a new understanding of language; we will see that "something must be for something to be said—there must be meaning to which our words point, not as . . . impositions, but as expressions of the meaning that stands out."[50] Language articulates the being of natural things—but nature allows some interpretations and disallows others, it constrains language.

Language is a gift that expresses the meaningful order of being, but expresses it indirectly and darkly. Words can gesture toward their source, but their source includes both the human who receives and interprets meaning as well as the thing that evokes a range of interpretations. Because of "the double discipline of the reality it confronts and the demands of those to whom it would speak,"[51] language is essentially suggestive rather than definitive. Words express that which is but cannot do so "with the same clarity and immediacy as in lived experience itself."[52] Yet lived experience must be articulated into words (and thoughts) if it is to be more than inchoate, fleeting, and immediately forgotten. The relationship between natural things, the experience of them, and the articulation of the experience into language is far more complex than the designative view suggests.

How does Kohak, as an heir of Faith, convince us that language is in fact expressive of the nature of the world? He simply uses language expressively. His text is filled with gentle, healing words: "inherent rhythms," "rhyme and reason," "integrated cycles," "continuity and periodicity of being," "harmony," "primordial and enduring presence," "immutable order," "revealing truths," "miraculous wonder," "invisible renewal," "deep solitude," "peace," "warmth." Kohak's text makes obvious the expressive function of all language. Moreover, he deploys the expressive function of language to evoke the reader's empathy—Kohak experiences nature as a meaningful whole and himself as a moral subject; his text rhetorically induces an "analogous experience."[53] Kohak's language resounds with the resemblances and similitudes of an enchanted natural world; it seeks to incite in the reader a longing for ontological comfort and to provide the means to achieve it.

A Preliminary Critique

While the holist critique of the management orientation to nature is often on target, the Kohakian alternative faces serious difficulties of its own. First, its rhetorical inducement of the moral sense of nature ignores the threatening and destructive aspects of nature. It is more difficult to "understand" drought, earthquakes, allergies, tornadoes, disease, and untimely death as meaningful parts of a moral order than it is to "understand" the quiet of the woods or the regularity of the tides. Until Kohak explicitly incorporates these troubling aspects of nature into his harmonious ontology, the view of nature as indifferent matter will remain a more convincing alternative.

Second, Kohak's view of nature is at odds with the modern institutional network that presupposes and engenders a demystified world. This would not in itself be a problem for Kohak if the structure of modern roles, beliefs, and practices were simply the result of a self-indulgent hubris or an infatuation with scientific theory. But our nontraditional roles, our scientific beliefs, and our technological practices are in some cases demonstrably superior to those that have preceded them. Kohak needs to show how his orientation to nature is not mere nostalgia for an enchanted view of the world that defeated itself earlier in Western history.[54] And he needs to consider the implications of his view of nature for individual rights, freedom of expression, medical advances, increases in literacy, and so forth.

Kohak would not deny that his philosophy of nature is incomplete or even inadequately justified. Indeed, he claims that given the intellectual finitude of humans, the orientation to nature one endorses is ultimately a matter of faith; it is simply not susceptible to complete justification or definitive proof.

All that can be said will not constitute an argument, nor will arguments convince. . . . All knowledge rests on faith. That faith, though, is neither arbitrary nor irrational. It is an expression of a vision.[55]

Kohak thus follows in the epistemological footsteps of picture-thoughts. Knowledge can be evocative only, never definitive. Trust or faith is necessary; we can get a glimpse of the moral order of nature, but not its blueprint.

From the perspective of natural holism, the real issue in the environmental debate is not how to devise and implement the most efficient method of pollution or polluter control but how to recognize the proper place of the human in the cosmos. The question "whether we shall conceive of ourselves as integrally continuous with the world . . . or as . . . strangers [thrown] into an alien medium"[56] is open, says Kohak, for "nature lends itself willingly to either interpretation."[57] Kohak's response to this question is based upon "an act of trust that the harmony of the embers that glow with the warmth of the human heart and the stars that proclaim the glory of God . . . is . . . the ultimate conclusion of deep thought."[58]

And Kohak helps us to see how the manager's response to the open question is also based on a faith—that technique is adequate to technologically induced problems. We begin to see as well that the evocative power of metaphor (rather than scientific proof) stands behind both the holist and the management positions. Supporting Kohak's vision are the metaphors "rhyme and reason," "periodicity of being," "primordial presence"; supporting the picture of nature as standing reserve are the metaphors "matter," "resources," "rights," "rationality." In spite of its flaws, Kohak's natural holism uncovers the tentative status of both the management and the harmonious holist assumptions about nature, self, and freedom.

A Reinvented Philosophy of Nature

Like Kohak, John Compton opposes the dominant understanding of nature as standing in reserve for human use. And modern science is again identified as an impediment to a natural holist alternative. But if it could be shown that modern science secretly relies upon a pretheoretical experience of nature wherein a harmony of self and nature is revealed, the case for holism would be advanced. Compton takes this tack and seeks to inform science of an unacknowledged debt to prescience. The philosophy of science, he hopes, could then become a "reinvented philosophy of nature" that grounds a new, ethical orientation to nature.

Compton, working within the tradition of Merleau-Ponty and others, begins with a phenomenological account of knowing. What makes both pretheoretical (lived experiential) and scientific knowing possible is a background of beliefs, conventions, perceptions, thoughts, impulses, ideals, principles, prejudices, weather- and temperature-induced feelings, bodily moods, and rhythms that offer the individual a bounded but diverse set of conceptual and action possibilities. This presuppositional framework is integral to knowing but cannot itself be known in full. It cannot become the explicit object of knowledge, for the only knowing available to humans is knowledge of a particularized object or group of objects that has been lifted out of the generalized background by the focus of attention. The background cannot itself be thematized all at once. The structure of any knowing is akin, then, to the structure of sight: to "see" is to focus on a particular item while necessarily blurring the field of vision in which it is set; to shift to another item requires the resubmergence of the first.

Pretheoretical knowing occurs almost automatically, at least without the conscious attempt to think. Its source is lived experience, its locus is perception. A normal human body, then, knows things before it theorizes them, but this knowledge is less complete and precise than scientific knowledge. Implicit, experiential knowledge of nature is pervasive and always there affecting thought and judgment, but its status as knowledge is suspect to the modern self because it is imprecise and inarticulate.

The status of scientific knowing, on the other hand, is as secure as its terms are precise. Yet scientific theory merely imitates lived experience—it accelerates, intensifies, and exaggerates the perceptual process of isolating items from within the field of experience. Scientific theories clarify lived knowledge, says Compton, at the risk of reification; they isolate the object of knowledge from its knowledge-context, fix it in a precise mathematical formula or statement of fact, and then typically deny that formulas and facts are abstractions from a holistic reality.

Scientific inquiry . . . is so technical . . . so pre-oriented to serve . . . interests in prediction and control, so selective . . . in its . . . assumptions, that we must wonder whether . . . it can provide . . . revealing knowledge of nature.[59]

Compton searches for a philosophy of nature that can walk the fine line between holistic but elusive knowledge and clear but reductive knowledge. Current scientific theory is incomplete because it does not acknowledge the insights of nonscientific experience of nature. But of what does "lived" knowledge consist? So far, Compton has articulated the process of pretheoretical knowing but not its special content. What insights about nature does a pretheoretical understanding reveal? Admitting the difficulty in articulating that which is pretheoretical, Compton offers the following "heuristically suggestive description" of what we know of nature by way of "bodily . . . activity with things as we seek to satisfy our needs and purposes."[60]

First, pretheoretical experience "says" that things of nature have some identifiable continuity and predictability. The objects of the lived natural world (events, processes, things, notions, and ideas) have recurrent constancies—for it is indeed possible to pick out ("perceive" or "know") one object from amidst all others. Certain relations among things also persist; they have characteristic (and in some cases even lawlike) ways of combining or interacting that cannot be explained away as a projection of a human "desire" for regularity.

This "desire" is more accurately described as a perceptual expectation. The continuity of things exists alongside and in collaboration with a perceptual expectation of regularity. Human bodies contribute to the continuity and unity of natural reality. Through them we identify and reidentify unities within the multiplicity of forms of the natural world. Lived experience of nature also speaks, then, of our perceptual participation in the constitution of things.

Compton describes this anticipatory apparatus as "the amorphous field of . . . spatiality and temporality, of moving and grasping, seeing and seeking."[61] This unifying field of the-body-as-it-interacts-with-nature operates at the intersubjective as well as the individual level, for

at the margin of each individual's experiences of things is the unstated, but assumed presence of other experiencers . . . Thus, the concrete unities-in-multiplicities . . . are . . . not only [mine] . . . but . . . *ours*.[62]

Actual, lived experience thus informs us of a dialectical relation between natural things and humans; we belong to each other because we exist only in conjunction with each other. Humans perceive and interpret nature through bodily organs that are themselves natural; individuals understand nature through categories handed down in a historical tradition that is itself conditioned by developments in natural history; individual humans, in conjunction with the intersubjective community, interpret nature because its flexibility and porousness render it susceptible to interpretation. Is the holistic picture beginning to emerge? Compton's cumbersome formulations seek to evoke the links of the great chain of being, all of which are located in experience.

More needs to be said about the "porousness" of natural objects. Actual experience is experience of something open-ended, with an indeterminacy that calls humans to a project of unification. But actual experience also teaches us that this project will never be fully successful or complete, for natural objects also have, so to speak, a life of their own. We will always be confronted by a startling exteriority as we experience the world. Humans find themselves over against but within nature. Within the perceptual-natural field, within the dialectical relationship between humans and nature, things become meaningful, but while human interpretation contributes to this meaning, it can never exhaust the perceived object.

Compton is not claiming that part of the meaning of an object is inherent and part derived from human interpretation—for all of the meaning of an object is bound up with its place in the lived world, that is, is essentially connected to the human experience of it. The point is, rather, that the object is more than its meaning. Of what that "more than" consists will always elude our grasp, for only mediated knowledge is available to humans. Compton does not dwell on what might be called the "raw material" of objects; he is not interested in unknowables. He does say that although the objects of lived reality are incompletely determinate and open to further determination, inviting human interpretation, they are at the same time experienced as resistant to us, as somewhat opaque, as already there before interpretation, as "always more than we know and ever surprising us."[63]

One could extend this claim to the human object, who as an embodied self is also a natural thing. For within the intention-bearing subject, the author of actions, is there not an "internal" exteriority that can take the form of inexplicable impulses, fury, depression, disease? Compton's position does not forbid this extension, but neither does he endorse it explicitly. For the acknowledgment of alien stuff within the self is at odds with his quest to elicit a primordial experience of being at home in the world.

Compton has argued that through lived experience we know that nature is made up of identifiable things that have continuity and predictability; that each of these things is essentially defined in relation to the others, including human others; and that these things have an open-endedness or indeterminacy so that even though humans participate in their existence, they are also surprised by them. What is remarkable about this list, says Compton, is that science comes up with a similar one when it seeks to determine the reality of a newly observed entity. In physics, for example, a new existant must be detected in several independent experiments (i.e., have identifiable continuity); or must interact with other known existants (i.e., be essentially relational); or must manifest a property hitherto only suspected (i.e., have an open-endedness that surprises).

Compton concludes that the theoretical constructs of natural science implicitly refer back to the knowing that is lived experience. To put it more precisely, perceptual experience puts limits upon what is recognizable by science as a part of nature. And once we see that science actually relies upon lived experience, pretheoretical intuitions of a harmonious, holistic connection between human selves and natural things will be more persuasive to a modern, managerial audience.

Let us compare Compton's version of natural holism with Kohak's. For Compton, what truth there is in the scientific orientation to nature does not lie in its ability to describe nature-in-itself. Compton cannot make sense of Kohak's notion of a "nature without reference to the presence of the effects of human or any other experiencing life."[64] The relevant gap for Compton is that between what we know of nature mediated through perception and what we know of nature mediated through theoretical constructs; Compton seeks to show us that these two modes of knowing are in implicit harmony. In contrast, Kohak is concerned with the gap between natural things as they are in themselves (intuitively available in the right natural setting) and the linguistic and institutional interpretation of them. For Kohak, we must express and unearth the truth of nature that lies waiting; Compton desires not so much that we speak what nature says, but that we acknowledge we always already do so. Moreover, the only nature available for expression is the already mediated nature of perception. Kohak's claim that there exists a holistic relationship between nature and self is grounded, he says, in an act of faith that this nature-in-itself is providential. Compton seeks to persuade us of natural holism by telling us to look no further than our own bodies, for therein lies evidence, although not "proof," of an ontological accord with nature.

In a sense, Compton's holism is more ambitious than Kohak's. It seeks to use the vocabulary of experience to dissolve the distinction between humans and the world in which they live. Because Compton understands this distinction as an overplayed convention at odds with authoritative, lived experience, it is often difficult to identify the subject of his sentences. Is "the world" acting or are "we" acting upon the world? Even his grammar blends the knower with the natural known. Or, to put it in phenomenological terms, even one's grammar must seek to demonstrate the primordial connection between nature and humans. The terms of Kohak's holism include nature-in-itself, the human experiencer of nature, and the relationship between them; for Compton all three terms merge into the natural-bodily-context-of-reality. And Compton would, if he could only find the vocabulary, dissolve even the hyphens.

But like Kohak, Compton makes claims about nature that, were they to be accepted, would necessitate radical changes in the technological orientation to nature now in ascendancy. Kohak claims that nature contains a moral order; Compton suggests not only that there are affinities between perceptual and theoretical knowing but that there is a holistic relation between human and nonhuman perceptual experience. "What is characteristic of embodied, intersubjective, world-related human life . . . is structurally analogous to what is found in other regions of the natural world."[65] Other holists have suggested this structural analogy, sometimes likening the human body to a self-regulating natural site:

The epidermis of the skin is . . . like a pond surface or a forest soil, not a shell so much as a delicate interpenetration. It reveals the self ennobled and extended rather than threatened as a part of the landscape . . . because the beauty and complexity of nature are continuous with ourselves.[66]

Also like Kohak, Compton does not seek to prove this philosophy of nature, for all claims about nature can only be suggestive possibilities. The details of the structural analogy between the human body and the natural order, an analogy that Compton uses to persuade that the cosmos is harmoniously ordered, are not specified. He does not try to defend fully his claim that nature forms a meaningful whole; he seeks merely to "point to some striking evidence of . . . [its] truth."[67] This evidence includes a phenomenological description of "lived experience" that uncovers what he hopes will appear as a remarkably fortuitous fit between anticipatory perception and porous objects.

The mode of argumentation of Kohak and Compton requires a sympathetic reader; its claim is that all conviction relies to a certain extent upon a prior disposition to believe. Kohak asks only that we listen to the evocative call of nature and metaphor; Compton asks us not to be convinced but merely to be open to the possibility of harmonious holism and to acknowledge the debt science owes to lived experience. And, as I have suggested above, Compton's phenomenological vocabulary is designed to carry some of the burden of persuasion.

Nature, Ethics, and Theology

And yet, Compton presents his position not as merely another alternative to the scientific conception of nature but as a morally superior alternative. The phenomenological approach "reminds us that . . . we could, in a reflective and empathetic way . . . enlarge the world we live to include responsiveness to life-world structures at other levels."[68] His approach is more ethical than the scientific alternative, for to inquire under the assumption of a harmonious natural holism is to foster the possibility of a respectful, nondestructive orientation to nature.

Through the environmental crisis, we have become painfully aware of the danger in attitudes of exploitation and domination reinforced by a philosophy which divests nature of meaning entirely.[69]

Let us grant that to assume a harmonious natural whole would result in a less destructive orientation to nature. Would that be enough to justify the assumption? There is some evidence, "in a broad sense empirical,"[70] to support the assumption of harmony, but there is also some experiential evidence to support the assumption of a world not designed for humans. Compton says that science must presuppose a harmonious holism if it is to have a nature-revealing and not merely instrumental or predictive quality—for if science was capable only of the latter, it could not "tell the difference between reality and useful fiction."[71]

Compton has, of course, thought of the possibility that we cannot "reveal" nature, that even if we could we would find it was not designed for us, and that human life is held together by nothing more than a series of useful fictions. But he rejects the possibility that our conceptual and perceptual acts do not "belong" as part of a rational universe; he rejects the possibility that primary experience, the phenomenological articulation of it, and scientific theorizing all have only a rough correspondence with the "outside" world; he rejects the possibility that the intensity and persistence of our wish for harmonious integration with nature might not imply any privileged ontological status for it.

Why does Compton make so much of very general and incomplete affinities between human and nonhuman being? He wants to do more than nudge science in the direction of ecology; the change in the orientation to nature he seeks requires stronger ammunition than systems theory. Compton needs God, and like Kohak, he borrows some of the power of the belief in God to strengthen the case for his philosophy of nature.

In "Science and God's Action in Nature," written earlier than "Re-inventing a Philosophy of Nature," Compton's explicit aim is to reconcile a theology of nature with natural science. He argues there that the alleviation of environmental crisis requires a revision of our orientation to nature, that the revision must affirm "intrinsic meaning and value in the natural order of which man is a part,"[72] and that this affirmation unfolds through notions of God, creation, providence, telos, and logos. Compton seeks to give these concepts "plausibility and applicability . . . in terms of our common experiences and . . . the scientific world view."[73] The essay contends that a tenable view of God's action in nature is one understood as analogous to the embodied human self engaged in lived experience of nature. This view of God is "consistent with Christian faith and may even be coherent with natural science."[74] The admission by theoretical physics and evolutionary theory that science can never fully explain matter (because it is indeterminate) is a sign, says Compton, that science has made room in its framework for a new conception of God—the modern God can find a home in the mystery of matter.

Compton's theological commitment provides the missing element
in a reinvented philosophy of nature based on lived experience.
Faith in God allow us to move from the mere possibility of harmonious holism, a possibility on a par with other views of the relationship between humans and nature, to the conviction of its truth.
There seems, then, to be a recurrent connection between theological
convictions and the orientation of natural holism. It seems unlikely
that holism could function even as an ideal without some residual
commitment to God as creator and designer of nature.

The Silent Partnership

We have explored the environmental debate through the lens of
Faith and Enlightenment and have discerned its contours, problem-
atics, and boundaries. The dominant understanding of nature as
standing reserve, because it has been unable to reverse the environmentally destructive path we are on, has spawned an alternative
understanding that demands respect for a nature to which we are
deeply indebted. And the preceding accounts of Kohak and Compton suggest that their respect for nature depends upon a harmonious
interpretation of lived experience and a faith in a providential universe.

We are now in a position to ask two questions that get at the
heart of the contemporary environmental debate: Is the only viable
alternative to the managerial orientation to nature one that assumes a harmonious holism? Is respect for nature impossible in a
world not designed for humans?

Both environmental management and natural holism answer yes.
And this affirmation uncovers a hidden affinity between these opponents, a bond of a silent partnership. Both collude to restrict the
range of debate—because natural holism is constituted in direct
response to its secular opponent, it cannot envision views of language, knowledge, and self that are both secular and respectful of
nature; because environmental management is designed to expose
natural holism as incongruous with modern beliefs and practices,

it cannot envision a respect for nature that is not nostalgia for an enchanted world.

Harmonious holism makes three basic claims:

(1) We must not treat nature as standing reserve because such treatment upsets the natural order and demeans humanity.

(2) Nature, humans, and reason harmonize at the most fundamental level of being.

(3) The moral power, the "must" of the first claim, is impossible without faith in the second.

Harmonious holism appears today as utopian, as abstract or disconnected from experience, because it is increasingly difficult for us to believe claim 2, that nature is predisposed to us. (The criticism that holism appears untenable in the modern world is persuasive.) But because we unconsciously believe claim 3, we, like Christopher Stone, reluctantly abandon the pursuit of respect for nature and return to some version of nature as standing reserve. If both harmonious holists and environmental managers believe that respect for nature is tied to a harmonious ontology, then holism will always be the defensive party in the debate.

Harmonious holism's opposition to the view of nature as standing reserve thus depends upon an increasingly fragile faith in the prospects for attunement. If one does not have this faith but wishes to preserve holism's insights about the interdependencies of humans and nature, one might seek a more practical science of ecology that deploys a systems-theory or holistic methodology. But this attempt to scientize holism has almost always entailed the eventual adoption of the fundamental assumptions of environmental management.

But perhaps the possibilities for an environmental ethic are broader than harmonious holism and environmental management. Perhaps there is a way to endorse claim 1, that nature must not be treated as standing reserve, without subscribing to claim 2, that the world is providential. Perhaps it is possible to center an environmental ethic around the belief that inside nature's affinity to human control resides a persistent resistance to it, a resistance that may not have any identifiable source.

Compton's point about the open-endedness of the objects of lived experience goes to the brink of this let-otherness-be position. There is an indeterminacy, he says, that both invites technical and conceptual imposition of unity and resists it, placing limits upon its duration. One could acknowledge that humans have functions, forms, and possibilities for action similar to those available to non-human nature, that nature "fits us" in so far as it provides the conditions of possibility for existence, and still reject the view that we were made for each other.

And it is consistent with the phenomenological evidence offered by Compton that humans are embodied selves, replete with affinities and with aspects accidental or adverse to human needs. We could endorse an essential but problematic relationality between humans and nature rather than an ontological harmony. Because of its theological commitments, natural holism does not appreciate this interpretation of the open-endedness of nature, and because of its anthropocentrism, neither does environmental management.

But what if we try to think beyond these terms of debate? What if we heed the critiques of each without being limited to the proffered set of affirmative positions? Hegel's insights about Faith and Enlightenment have helped to expose the impasse of the current debate, but the task of exploring the excluded turf still remains. Perhaps if we challenge the claim that is shared by managers and harmonizers alike, that respect for nature requires a belief in an "eidetic structure of being" (claim 3), we could then transcend the impasse governing contemporary environmental debates. I take up this challenge further in chapter 4.

NOTES

1. Heidegger describes the modern orientation to nature in this way:
Everywhere everything is ordered to stand by, to be immediately at hand, indeed to stand there just so that it may be on call for a further ordering. . . . We call it the standing-reserve.

(*The Question Concerning Technology*, p. 17)
For a discussion of "standing-reserve," see that essay and "The Age of the World Picture" in *The Question Concerning Technology and Other Essays*, trans. William Lovitt (New York: Harper Colophon, 1977).

2. There are two overlapping types of environmental management. The

first is made up primarily of the work of environmental economists and includes positions both opposed to and defensive of economic growth. See, for example, Harold Barnett and Chandler Morse, *Scarcity and Growth* (Baltimore: Johns Hopkins University Press, 1963); Wilfred Becherman, *In Defense of Economic Growth* (London: Jonathan Cape, 1974); Partha Dasgupta, *The Control of Resources* (Cambridge: Harvard University Press, 1982); A. Myrick Freeman, *The Benefits of Environmental Improvement* (Baltimore: Resources for the Future, 1979); Dennis Meadows, Donella Meadows, J. Randers, W. W. Behrens, *The Limits to Growth* (New York: Universe, 1972).

The second is made up primarily of the work of political scientists. See, for example, Peter Bohm, *Deposit-Refund Systems* (Baltimore: Resources for the Future, 1981); Garrett Hardin and John Baden, eds., *Managing the Commons* (San Francisco: W. H. Freeman, 1977); Allen Kneese and Charles Schultze, *Pollution, Prices, and Public Policy* (Washington, D.C.: Brookings Institution, 1975); Norman J. Vig and Michael E. Draft, *Environmental Policy in the 1980s* (Washington, D.C.: Congressional Quarterly, 1984).

3. As examples of the natural holist approach to environmentalism, see John Cobb, "Ecology, Ethics, and Theology," in *Toward a Steady-State Economy*, ed. Herman Daly (San Francisco: W. H. Freeman, 1973); John Compton, "Re-inventing a Philosophy of Nature," *Review of Metaphysics* 33 (September 1979); Erazim Kohak, *The Embers and the Stars* (Chicago: University of Chicago Press, 1984); C. S. Lewis, *The Abolition of Man* (New York: Macmillan, 1947); Harold Schilling, "The Whole Earth Is the Lord's: Toward a Holistic Ethic," in *Earth Might Be Fair*, ed. Ian Barbour (Englewood Cliffs, N.J.: Prentice-Hall, 1972); E. F. Schumacher, *Small Is Beautiful* (New York: Harper and Row, 1975).

4. Kneese and Schultze, *Pollution, Prices, and Public Policy*, pp. 24–25.

5. Society was "conventionalized" by Enlightenment. Tradition could no longer ground society, for tradition was a reification—it insinuated an enduring unity of past and present that simply did not exist. Conventional society, on the other hand, is a human contrivance self-conscious of its nonnatural, controversial, and controvertible form. As traditions and customs were replaced by reflective norms and rational policies, the social order became susceptible to techniques of administrative rationalization.

6. My account of the regulation and market-incentive approaches draws from Kneese and Schultze, which I consider a paradigmatic example of environmental management.

7. Barnett and Morse, *Scarcity and Growth*, p. 12.

8. John Passmore, *Man's Responsibility for Nature* (London: Duckworth, 1974), p. 177.

9. Barnett and Morse, p. 7.

10. Barnett and Morse, p. 10.

11. Barnett and Morse, p. 10.

12. Passmore, p. 33.

13. Passmore, p. 179.

14. Passmore, p. 180.

15. Christopher Stone, *Should Trees Have Standing?* (Los Altos, Calif.: William Kaufmann, 1974). Stone's position, designed as a critique of both types of environmental management, still shares their fundamental assumptions about nature, self, and freedom. Because Stone seeks a broader, more critical perspective and yet remains within the management paradigm, I chose his book as the focus of my critique of environmental management. Stone is no straw man; his is one of the more theoretically sophisticated versions of environmental management. See also Passmore; Robin Attfield, *The Ethics of Environmental Concern* (Oxford: Basil Blackwell, 1983); W. F. Frankena, "Ethics and the Environment," in *Ethics and the Problems of the Twenty-First Century*, ed. K. E. Goodpaster and K. M. Sayre (Notre Dame, Ind.: Notre Dame University Press, 1979).

16. Stone, p. 178.

17. Stone, p. 6.

18. Stone, p. 9, note 26.

19. Stone, p. 28.

20. Stone, p. 19, note 53.

21. Stone, p. 31.

22. Stone, p. 17.

23. For an excellent critique of this model, see John Rodman, "The Liberation of Nature," *Inquiry* 20 (1977).

24. Evidence of this trend is the breeding of animals more and more according to marketing, packaging, and distribution imperatives, as well as the emergence of animal-rights groups protesting this practice.

25. Stone, p. 20.

26. Stone, p. 48.

27. Stone, p. 16.

28. Frankena distinguishes between instrumental value and inherent value, where the former refers to the concrete uses of a natural thing and the latter refers to the more subtle worth a thing has through its ability to inspire, fascinate, spiritually heal, or aesthetically please us ("Ethics and the Environment"). But neither does this distinction challenge an instrumental orientation to nature.

29. Attfield, p. 146.

30. Attfield, p. 160.

31. Passmore, p. 184.

32. Quoted in Passmore, p. 107.

33. Paul Shepard, "Introduction: Ecology and Man—A Viewpoint," in *The Subversive Science*, ed. Paul Shepard and Daniel McKinley (Boston: Houghton Mifflin, 1969), p. 9.

34. Frank E. Egler, "Pesticides—in Our Ecosystem," in *The Subversive Science*, p. 246.

35. Passmore, p. 183.

36. C. S. Lewis, another natural holist, offers a different version of this criticism. He argues that the more we attempt to master nature, the larger the number of technical devices we create. The more technical devices in existence, the more possibilities for some people to be deprived of them by others. Thus, he concludes, any increase in human power over nature is always an increase in some human's power over other humans. "Each [technical] advance leaves him [humanity] weaker as well as stronger. In every victory, besides being the general who triumphs, he is also the prisoner who follows the triumphal car" (*The Abolition of Man*, p. 323).

37. Kohak, *The Embers and the Stars*, p. 5.

38. Kohak, *The Embers and the Stars*, p. 49.

39. Kohak, *The Embers and the Stars*, p. 6.

40. Kohak, *The Embers and the Stars*, p. 74.

41. Kohak, *The Embers and the Stars*, p. 12.

42. Kohak, *The Embers and the Stars*, p. 17.

43. Kohak, *The Embers and the Stars*, p. 23.

44. Kohak, *The Embers and the Stars*, p. 35.

45. Kohak, *The Embers and the Stars*, p. 22.

46. Kohak, *The Embers and the Stars*, p. 35.

47. Kohak, *The Embers and the Stars*, p. 29.

48. Kohak, *The Embers and the Stars*, p. 57.

49. Kohak, *The Embers and the Stars*, p. 42.

50. Kohak, *The Embers and the Stars*, p. 48.

51. Kohak, *The Embers and the Stars*, p. 68.

52. Kohak, *The Embers and the Stars*, p. 48.

53. Kohak, *The Embers and the Stars*, p. 64.

54. For an account of these defects, see Hans Blumenberg, *The Legitimacy of the Modern Age* (Cambridge: MIT Press, 1983), pt. II.

55. Kohak, *The Embers and the Stars*, p. 175.

56. Kohak, *The Embers and the Stars*, p. 8.

57. Kohak, *The Embers and the Stars*, p. 125.

58. Kohak, *The Embers and the Stars*, pp. 126–27.

59. Compton, "Re-inventing the Philosophy of Nature," p. 6.

60. Compton, "Re-inventing," pp. 7–8.

61. Compton, "Re-inventing," p. 9.

62. Compton, "Re-inventing," pp. 9–10.

63. Compton, "Re-inventing," p. 9.

64. Compton, "Re-inventing," p. 22.

65. Compton, "Re-inventing," p. 24.

66. Shepard, p. 2.

67. Compton, "Re-inventing," p. 12.
68. Compton, "Re-inventing," p. 25.
69. Compton, "Re-inventing," p. 28.
70. Compton, "Re-inventing," p. 5.
71. Compton, "Re-inventing," p. 16.
72. John Compton, "Science and God's Action in Nature," in *Earth Might Be Fair*, p. 33.
73. Compton, "Science," p. 37.
74. Compton, "Science," p. 43.

CHAPTER 3

THE JURIDICAL STATE,
THE CONSENSUAL STATE,
THE ATTUNED STATE

CHAPTER 2 revealed ways in which two readily available orientations to nature, Enlightenment-inspired environmental management and Faith-inspired natural holism, are both seriously flawed. While management reveals defects in holism and holism those in management, neither provides an adequate affirmative stance; each addresses inadequacies in its opponent but is ill-equipped to address those in itself. Chapter 3 explores the ways in which this Faith-Enlightenment problematic surfaces in theories of the modern, Western state.

This chapter discusses two Enlightenment theories of the state—the individualist, juridical state of Theodore Lowi and the collectivist, consensual state of Jürgen Habermas—and one Faith theory, the attuned state of Charles Taylor. Each theory offers a critique of the existing state and then a new model relationship of government, economy, and citizenry.

Each theory of the state is concerned with freedom; the pursuit of a particular conception of freedom fosters an accompanying theory of the state. For an Enlightenment theory, in either its individualist or collectivist mode, freedom is the exercise of self-assertion in a world where humans can in principle be in charge—thus freedom requires self-conscious, rational control over the social order. For a Faith or attuned theory, freedom is human accommodation to a world always partly beyond human control—freedom thus requires a social order in harmony with the larger world in which it is situated.

The Paradox of Political Freedom

The individualist theory of the state can be seen as a response to Hegel's critique of absolute freedom. This theory is alert to the dangers within collectivism: an emphasis on a general will places a heavy burden on civic virtue, and excessive faith in the possibility of rational, collective self-government risks the absolute terror of authoritarianism. In response to this, the individualist theory locates the realm of freedom primarily within the individual, securing a niche for freedom in production or consumption choices; it minimizes citizens' identification with the state by defining the state as technical coordinator of diverse private needs; and it strengthens controls on bureaucratic power in order to reduce the areas of life subject to official regulation.

But the collectivist theory identifies a corollary set of dangers in the individualist theory: to confine freedom to an economic ghetto is to risk turning citizens into mere consumers; to minimize citizens' identification with the state may be to weaken further the legitimacy of a state already conceived as hostage to a privately controlled economy; to define the state as technical coordinator is to further technocracy at the expense of democracy; to see bureaucratic power as disabling freedom obscures the connection between freedom and collective action. In response, collectivism attempts to rework the dialectic of absolute freedom and terror, hoping that a more sophisticated understanding of the dangers of collective decision-making can prevent the abuse of state power and still fulfill the legitimacy and coordination needs of a modern democratic state.

The individualist fears the political oppression that results from attempts to collectivize, and the collectivist fears the oppression of politics that results from individualism. And if we step outside this debate, we see that the danger each sees in the other is the same danger—authoritarianism and technocracy are both forms of excessive social control. According to the theory of the attuned state, this danger stems from a Promethean commitment to human mastery of an ultimately rationalizable world. Both Enlightenment theories assume that the state with the greatest potential for freedom is the one with the most fully mastered social order. Understanding individualism and collectivism differently from the way they appear in the critique of each by the other, the attuned state sees both as imprisoned within a paradox of political freedom that neither understands.

The paradox is this: political freedom requires a life lived partly in common through the vehicle of the state (through norms, policies, and agencies that express and implement the public will), but any state strong enough to achieve public goals (for the sake of freedom) also risks the authoritarian or technocratic abuse of political power (and thus fosters unfreedom). Enlightenment theories aspire to

attain a state wherein the radical contradiction which exists between a universality pursued by the state and the particularity and caprice which it evinces in reality would be resolved. The evil is that this aspiration is not within our reach.[1]

The internal alliance between social order and bureaucratic control illustrates the paradox of political freedom. A good state must maintain order and coordinate a diverse set of functions. And because both the individualist and the collectivist believe that the best order is the most thoroughly rationalized, they are drawn (the individualist reluctantly) to actions that further diversify state responsibilities and extend the mechanisms of bureaucratic regulation. But these actions increase citizens' resentment of impersonal bureaucratic treatment and monitoring, a resentment that undermines the social order.

A second illustration of the paradox is the link between the pursuit of collective identity and intolerance of heterodoxy. A good state must instill (or evoke) in its citizens a sense of allegiance, but the unification of the citizenry entails the marginalization of some groups. The collectivist pursues an integrated political will through rational public discourse, but the very pursuit of consensus denigrates persons with politically incorrect views. Individualism tries to avoid the collectivist intolerance by refusing to endorse a politics of the common good; it believes itself neutral regarding the content of "the good life." But individualism too presupposes some notion of normality and the public interest and thus has standards of valuation favorable to those citizens who conform most closely to them.

An individualist theory of the state might attempt to transform the paradox into a procedural compromise between particular interests and the public interest. This compromise typically exempts the economy, the realm of particular interests, from the clutches of the public-interest-bearing state. But this exemption produces a state unable to realize the public interest, and in such a state the individual is less free, for individual freedom is linked to collective freedom.

The internal connection between my sense of individual freedom and my belief that the state is the locus of effective, collective action is this: if I find certain role requirements to be both conventional and unjustifiably restrictive, if I can neither reconstitute them by myself nor adopt others, *my freedom is still potentially intact if we can collectively reconstitute them should others come to agree with my assessment.* Unless the state could (if it would) alter such conventions, then its unfreedom contributes to mine.[2]

A state bound by imperatives flowing from a privately controlled economy is unfree in the sense that citizens' ability to reconstitute burdensome rules and roles is diminished.

A collectivist theory might attempt to overcome the paradox by ensuring that the state embodies rationally endorsed norms. It would thus be no more dangerous than the legitimately derived definition of the common good. This attempt, however, will be accompanied by an interminable debate over the content of the common good or over the sheer possibility of rational consensus.

The standing potential of the abuse of state power through official control or through social persecution of difference is ineliminable as long as humans remain political and continue to possess the (political-public) capacity for (political-public) freedom. The paradox of the modern state, according to the attuned theory of the state, is that the realization of political freedom is tied to the standing potential for destroying it.

The paradox can never be dissolved completely, says the theorist of attunement, but its grip could be relaxed were we to eschew the Promethean orientation of both Enlightenment theories. Both the individualist and the collectivist demand too much—the social order can never be as rationalized as they desire, and we can never be fully in charge of the order of our own making. Why then not pursue a social order that is simpler and requires less control and coordination? The theory of the attuned state acknowledges the limits to social order and human mastery and then advocates a modest, decentralized steady state where humans need not try to be in full charge. The attuned state pursues not continual economic growth and social coordination but accommodation to the inherent limits to economic growth and social control.

As one who understands the dialectic of Faith and Enlightenment would expect, however, the theory of the attuned state is not itself flawless. It presupposes views of self and nature difficult to sustain within modern life. It adopts a view of nature and self similar to that found in the harmonious holism investigated in chapter 2.

I turn now to the first of these three theories of the state.

The Juridical State

Every theory of the state is guided by an ideal. According to Lowi, the individualist ideal, or the true end of liberalism, is a juridical democracy with a neo-laissez-faire economy.

The ideal state is juridical, governed by formal law. Informal bargaining, "politicking," is replaced by formal procedures that shift the balance of political power toward Congress and the judiciary and away from corporate lobbyists and government bureaucrats. A thoroughly legalized and rigorously disciplined legislature can then produce policies whose intent is clear and whose applications are clearly specified.

Too much of currert American policy expresses only "broad and noble sentiments, giving almost no direction . . . but imploring executive power, administrative expertise, and interest-group wisdom."[3] By assuming that policy resulting from these unregulated influences is by definition just, we eschew the formulation of principles of justice.

Considerations of justice . . . cannot be made unless a deliberate and conscious attempt was made to derive the [public] action from a preexisting general rule or moral principle governing such a class of actions. Therefore, any . . . regime that makes a virtue of avoiding such rules puts itself outside the context of justice.[4]

While Lowi's "juridical approach does not dictate a particular definition of justice, of virtue, or of the good life,"[5] the politics of government by law fosters a healthy consideration of them.

The juridical state strengthens the role of Congress (in order to allow for greater clarification of and consistency among public acts), but it does not disempower local government. Because national directives make clear the responsibilities of local authorities, self-monitoring helps to reduce central control. Federal oversight, when necessary, is less intrusive, for judgments of success or failure can be straightforward when standards have been made explicit beforehand.

Moreover, government by formal law enables citizens to assign responsibility for public policies (the law has an overt, formally recorded history rather than a genealogy of discretion, accidents, and secret deals), and it enables the state to rationalize its policy agenda (law-derived policy can be modified, in known and regular ways) to adjust to complex and changing circumstances. A juridical state is best able to simplify and systematize policy-as-law, to produce, ultimately, a "unified code."[6] After all, "legality and efficiency tend to go together."[7]

But Lowi's ideal state is also democratic, with opportunities for public participation. Citizens are encouraged to "bargain on the rule," to participate in an open, public, reflective debate about the aim, import, and implication of a piece of legislation. Access is both ensured and delimited by law. Bargaining on the rule is desirable during the formulation stage of policy, but because well-formed policy includes instructions for its own administration, little bargaining is justified during the implementation process. In a similar manner, special economic interests are given access only to open congressional forums where their interests appear clearly as corporate and not public ones. Corporate lobbying power is also minimized through the juridical requirement of precise and overt policy intentions: "In many cases the powerful would be immobilized if they had to articulate what they were going to do before they did it."[8]

Government by law also lessens the possibility of covert bureaucratic power. Careful laws with definitive aims allow Congress to control expenditures of public agencies and to check administrative discretion, a major source of policy inconsistency and public cynicism toward government.

It is the broad grant of power without standards that leads to bargaining, unanticipated commitments, and . . . confusions that are the essence of bureaucratic irresponsibility and the illegitimate state.[9]

But, says Lowi, government by law is insufficient to restore democratic liberalism. As the undesirable side effects of capitalism have grown, the liberal state has been drawn into an economic role that has undermined its commitment to democratic participation and the public interest. Lowi argues that the state's orientation to the economy, as well as its orientation to legislation, must be modified.

In order for a modern state to coordinate rationally a large range of purposes, it must control "at least some of the strategic resources and networks in the economy."[10] The American state has responded to this coordination imperative not, as other welfare states have done, by socializing production or banking, but by socializing risk. Examples of the socialization of risk include regulations that protect established firms by limiting new entrants into the competition (the role of the Civil Aeronautics Board) and federal guarantees of loans to private investors (the role of the Emergency Loan Guarantee

Board in the Lockheed case). In 1978 the American government had potential obligations for $368 billion worth of private investments.[11]

This form of public economic intervention, where the government underwrites the organizational and fiscal stability of industries or corporations deemed important to the economy, creates a large class of private units in a state of "permanent receivership." Lowi is highly critical of this development. Because receivership typically requires no immediate transfer of funds, but only a pledge to assume debts if the enterprise fails, the government agency underwriting the risk can escape official Treasury or congressional clearance. There is thus both too little opportunity for public debate about which firms to insure and too much administrative discretion once firms have been chosen. A close internal relationship between ostensibly public agencies or committees and their private clienteles is established, which further reduces the accountability of receivership funds and firms.

Once a firm has joined the ranks of permanent receivership, it gains a structural advantage over newer firms, for the initial state intervention entails a certain obligation for the state to protect its investment. Thus, permanent receivership discriminates against innovative (and usually small) enterprises that could increase the competitiveness of an economic sector; it allows "economically irrational uses of resources by encouraging expansion beyond demand or . . . retention of inefficient firms or processes."[12]

Neo-laissez-faire, Lowi's substitute for permanent receivership, would combine "a substantial deflation of government in general with a strengthening of certain aspects of government in particular."[13] It would

radicalize economy and society . . . by an . . . abnegation of government power. . . . Multinational . . . corporations could probably be jolted back into more actual price competition if the hundreds of protections . . . lodged in our public policy were suddenly eliminated.[14]

A neo-laissez-faire state would still intervene in the economy for the sake of justice and the public interest (as these terms will be defined in the reformed political process), but the state would reduce the number of economic activities deemed the responsibility of government.

Under neo-laissez-faire, many discretionary economic programs would be abolished and others placed in a defensive position. Nondiscretionary fiscal policies—such as shifts in the money supply, the level of government investment, and tax laws—would be strengthened. Federal police power to regulate economic activity destructive of the public interest would expand, but such regulation would be clear in intent and limited in scope. "If there is . . . unacceptable distribution of income, . . . irrational use of resources, . . . water or air pollution or racial inequality, then [we] ought to be able to identify rather precisely"[15] their sources and remedies.

A Preliminary Critique

Lowi's procedural polity and neo-laissez-faire economy represent the individualist version of Enlightenment rationalism. Habermas's faith in the possibility of rational consensus represents the collectivist version. Before I provide an account of Habermas's affirmative theory of the state, I will sketch how his consensual state is a critique of the Lowian. Then, in order to expose a different set of flaws in the Lowian ideal, I anticipate briefly the critique by the theory of the attuned state. This last critique, which applies to the Habermasian ideal as well as the Lowian, focuses upon the Promethean project of human mastery.

From a Habermasian perspective, Lowi's defense of neo-laissez-faire is insufficient, even on his own terms. Lowi calls his attack on permanent receivership a protest "against the existing state as supportive of organized capitalism,"[16] a recognition of capitalism's oligarchical tendencies, and an assault on the bloated and irresponsible bureaucratic state. Yet neo-laissez-faire preserves the fundamental structures of capitalism and itself anticipates "a large though altered state apparatus."[17] But, the collectivist will ask, if Lowi is willing to invest the state with extensive coordination and planning powers, why does he exclude the possibility of neosocialism? Would not some version of socialism afford even greater corporate accountability?

Lowi's first objection to socialism, that a socialist transformation of the political economy would not necessarily remedy the problems of rule by professional expertise and administrative discretion, is weak, for neither necessarily does capitalism, in ways that Lowi himself has shown. Why couldn't the juridical control of discretionary power be applied to a socialized economy? Lowi's second objection, that the radical shift to socialism would entail an unacceptable (even if interim) sacrifice of civil liberties, is more serious but is still insufficient to reject all versions of socialism. State capitalism, by generating economic privileges, itself compromises civil liberties, as Lowi himself admits. Lowi is willing to live with these compromises but not with the socialist tendency to suppress individual liberty. Thus, Lowi's state provides for certain niches for purely individual activity, that is, activity structurally unavailable for deployment as a means to a larger political plan—and socialism cannot do this.

But from a collectivist perspective, Lowi's faith that capitalism can best protect individual liberty is unjustified. Lowi acknowledges that a neo-laissez-faire approach will give relatively free reign to private economic units, and that is why he also insists upon a state with strong juridical procedures designed to regulate corporate political influence. But Lowi doesn't see, Habermas will argue, that exposing corporate demands to the light of juridical procedure (while leaving the capitalist structure of the economy intact) may result in the crystallization and empowerment of corporate demands. Corporate priorities may be persuasively presented as necessary to the very existence of the social order rather than, as Lowi hopes, revealed as unjust and at odds with the public interest. And once corporate demands appear as social necessities, the state is obliged to channel public resources in their service—this fiscal burden may force the state to reduce expenditures on social programs less obviously central to the maintenance of the system. If the juridical state concedes to the economic imperatives of corporate capitalism and these imperatives require sacrifices on the part of certain politically expendable groups, then juridical capitalism might function to specify, clearly and precisely, the ways in which those sacrifices must be enforced and those evaders penalized.

Finally, the collectivist will take issue with Lowi's very conception of the state. Conceiving the state primarily in terms of the laws it makes, Lowi's analysis does not give serious attention to citizens' identification with the state or to the way the state is called upon as a locus of collective freedom. Lowi thus underestimates and misconstrues the modern problem of legitimacy:

(1) For Lowi the first source of the legitimacy problem is the perpetuation of permanent receivership: if the state continues to underwrite the private economy it will have trouble securing allegiance from citizens who recognize that public funds enhance the private gain of already privileged groups. This source of discontent is to be remedied through neo-laissez-faire, which greatly restricts the ranks of receivership as it subjects them to greater public accountability. But there is reason to believe, as suggested above, that neo-laissez-faire entails a state too weak to control the corporate economy.

(2) The second potential source of legitimation problems, according to Lowi, is ambiguous laws and bad procedures, for when no one can be sure whether a policy has been successful in carrying out an intention, public actions appear pointless or a smoke screen for the real, private sources of power. This threat to legitimacy is to be remedied through juridical democracy, but Habermas will argue that it is doubtful that procedures are ever sufficient to induce allegiance to the state.

For the theorist of the attuned state, many of these objections are valid, but the collectivist does not uncover a more profound error in the juridical ideal that is the source of its specific flaws—a Promethean orientation to the world. Put another way, juridical democracy and neo-laissez-faire economics reproduce the mistakes and dangers of the utilitarianism of Enlightenment.

Let us recall Hegel's discussion of the Enlightenment principle of utility. Enlightenment attempted to replace religious bases of value with utility, a standard that presupposed the intrinsic value of humans and a great faith in the power of reason. Hegel argued that utility was a standard of value whose realization would undermine its presuppositions: to determine value through utility is to view the world instrumentally, and this instrumental orientation would spread to humans themselves, the very beings exalted as the measure of all things. Although the faith in reason was great enough to include the belief that human reflectiveness would prevent this overextension of utility, as pure reason triumphed over traditional supports and limits, the assumption of the self-limiting character of reason was increasingly called into question.

Lowi, although he is concerned with politics more than with ethical theory, reenacts this earlier failed drama in his theory of the state. According to the theorist of the attuned state, the Enlightenment valorization of use value and its faith in the self-sufficiency of reason become, respectively, Lowi's capitulation to economic imperatives and his faith in a self-correcting juridical procedure. Just as Enlightenment sought both utility and respect for persons, Lowi wants both an efficient capitalist economy and the public interest. This tension between the desire for rational control and the desire for individual dignity manifests itself also in Lowi's pursuit of both a rationalized bureaucracy and a loosened regulation of citizens and in his pursuit of both a high-tech state and a democratically controlled state.

Lowi's thought moves within the parameters set by Enlightenment: his legal-procedural approach treats as unproblematic the Enlightenment view of reason; his conception of freedom as mastery has not explored the underside of the attempt to rationalize society; and his commitment to an economy of growth expresses his acceptance of an Enlightenment view of nature and human satisfaction. I have already touched upon Lowi's proceduralism; his commitment to mastery and economic growth is just as central to his theory. For Enlightenment, nature is disenchanted matter to be harnessed for human goals; for Lowi, these goals are upward mobility and an increasing material standard of living. If nature is matter, then the impact the pursuit of growth has upon nature is troublesome only insofar as it interferes with the pursuit. If Enlightenment equates human freedom with being in charge of the world, if the world separate from humans is thought to contain no intrinsic value, and if human well-being is seen as dependent upon the conversion of nature into useful objects, then economic growth is likely to be seen as an essential ingredient in human freedom and happiness.

This commitment to economic growth is problematic, according to the theorist of attunement, for the requirements of economic growth, like the standard of utility, tend to infest other social realms. The standards of efficiency, competition, and profit penetrate the human relation to nature as it becomes standing reserve; they shape politics as it is reduced to questions of international competition and stimulation of consumption rather than of the good life to be shared in common; they permeate ethical life as commercial success becomes its guide; they infect education as it becomes technical training for employment in growth industries rather than a study of liberal arts; they contaminate play as it becomes leisure in opposition to work, something to be "spent wisely"; and they infiltrate family and community as stability is undermined by the geographical mobility that is a condition of employment.

Lowi's commitment to mastery also prevents him from full awareness of the danger of strengthening the bureaucracy. Juridical democracy takes steps toward a perfected bureaucracy: one that runs according to the book, with a minimum of inefficiency, administrative discretion, and loopholes. The congressional debates fostered by juridical democracy can result in normative standards for a policy rather than loose sentiments, but the power of bureaucracy has sources other than the discretion to interpret policy intent. It stems also from its technical expertise, an expertise difficult to duplicate in legislators or citizens participating in bargaining on the rule. This technocratic power, says the attuned theorist, is likely to increase rather than decrease if we continue to seek technological mastery of the world.

Lowi criticizes pluralism for its technocratic conception of the public interest and for eschewing moral concerns (thus rendering politics incapable of justice), but his own affirmative position cannot redress these flaws. A theory of the state concerned about the antidemocratic implications of technocratic power could seek to reverse the need for increasingly complex technologies, pursuing "appropriate technology," technology more easily controlled, understood, and afforded by citizens while still providing a comfortable life. But this alternative requires changes—in the sanctity of economic growth, in the commitment to large-scale industry, in the organization of production, and in the acceptability of the largely unhindered accumulation of private wealth. And none of these changes is on Lowi's agenda.

The last two, however, are on Habermas's. I turn now to the theory of the consensual state, with an eye toward the way it improves upon Lowi's ideal and yet is still subject to the charge of Prometheanism.

The Consensual State

Habermas's theory of the state begins with the insight that although states throughout history have had to justify themselves to their populace, the burden of legitimation is especially heavy in modern states, for social arrangements formerly seen as natural[18] have become products of conscious policies in need of more explicit justification. In a truly legitimate modern state, these manifold policies distribute socially produced wealth equally. But advanced capitalist states are founded on the very opposite premise, on an asymmetrical class compromise. They have, then, this particular legitimation dilemma: they must justify policy as contributing to the common good, yet they cannot tolerate the democratic processes that could truly do so, for these processes threaten to expose the illegitimate compromise.

Capitalist states, says Habermas, have responded to this dilemma with a variety of pseudo-legitimation mechanisms: they institute formal but not substantive democracy (juridical democracy is one of these attempts); they emphasize the material rewards capitalism provides; they foster an ideological system supportive of capitalism. While the first two mechanisms appear robust, the last is an increasingly fragile bulwark against a legitimation crisis. The capitalist state has special difficulty motivating citizens to endorse personal aims compatible with the privately incorporated economy and to accept sacrifices required by it. More important, the state is losing its ability to convince citizens that there are opportunities

within the order for a meaningful life, one that includes the possibility of "a mimetic relation with nature; . . . solidarity outside . . .
the immediate family; . . . experience . . . giving scope to imagination as well as spontaneity."[19] For Habermas, a legitimate state
is not only economically efficacious, it makes self-realization possible. Juridical democracy does not take on this task, for Lowi mistakenly assumes that the American state is already on firm
existential ground.

Psychological allegiance to the capitalist state, says Habermas,
has depended upon two ideologies, "civil privatism" and "familial-
vocational privatism." The first is an orientation to politics that
sees the state as legitimate simply if it ensures the economic pre-
conditions for occupational achievement and accumulation of
wealth. The second "consists in the family orientation with developed interests in consumption and leisure . . . and in a career orientation suitable to status competition."[20] Both forms of privatism
focus attention toward the efficiency of state administration and
away from the ability of the state to act as a center of self-fulfillment, collective identity, and justice.

This privatism relied heavily upon precapitalist or religious traditions. "Capitalist societies were always dependent on cultural
boundary conditions they could not themselves reproduce."[21] The
capitalist citizen's indifference to the substantive ends of a social
order relies upon a traditional sense of duty to authority; her attitude toward economic achievement and material accumulation is
tied to religiously inculcated values of honesty, self-discipline, re-
nunciation of immediate gratification, fatalism, and the saving
power of hard work. Habermas claims that because these supportive
traditions now coexist within a relativistic and scientific age
(rather than within the solid worldview of Christianity or even
nineteenth-century liberalism), allegiance to them and thus to the
privatism they engender is fading. Capitalism, then, is losing the
motivational ground beneath its feet.

Today the threat posed by the decline of privatism does not seem
as grave as Habermas presents it, for the educational-occupational
system of capitalism seems quite firmly intact. Whether this is due
to a robust civil and familial-vocational privatism or to resignation

to fate amidst the decline of privatism is not certain, but I will argue the latter.

The clamor to participate in the most lucrative of the available occupational roles seems stronger than ever. But while overt participation in the educational-occupational system continues, this participation is not of the sort that can legitimate the capitalist state. We see a high degree of participation, at least among the American middle classes, but it is a participation easily divorced from allegiance to the state. Many may strive to succeed within existing structures, but many are also motivated to cut corners, evade standards, resist directives, and cheat within them.

Individuals are disciplining themselves to fit a corporate mold, and they experience (with varying degrees of self-consciousness) self-discipline as a reduction of self, as a burdensome imposition, albeit one necessary to get along in this world. In support of Habermas's claim about the legitimacy crisis, it does seem that this self-disciplinary response is itself precarious: participation in the system is accompanied by doubts about the meaningfulness of participation, as the end it is supposed to serve (a high-paying, high-status job) is ever-elusive and recognized as such, or is attained and experienced as unsatisfying or demeaning.

To summarize this revision of Habermas's account of privatism, participants in the occupational-educational system are in a bind. On the one hand, they see the economic organization of society as contingent, for they know it to be specific to this historical time and place. On the other hand, this contingency (because it is entrenched in consumption possibilities, available occupational roles, advertisements, etc.) acts upon them with the force of necessity or fate. Many members of the capitalist state respond, then, with the response appropriate to an arbitrary fate—they grudgingly oblige.

This modest revision builds upon rather than refutes Habermas's argument as a whole. And it coheres with his next move, to show how the capitalist state has attempted to develop new grounds for the motivation it requires. These substitutes include, on the one hand, modern religion, science, and utilitarianism, and on the other, modernist art and self-conscious norms. Both sets fail, says Habermas, as functional equivalents of privatism and its traditions, although for different reasons. The first set contains essentially inadequate sources of existential comfort and fulfillment, and the elements of the second set, while able to provide meaningful interpretations of the world and outlets for self-expression, cannot legitimate a *capitalist* state. Instead, they expose the tension between capitalism and the good life; the meaning they offer is mostly countercultural. Modernist art and the pursuit of self-conscious norms are, however, compatible with an anticapitalist, consensual state.

Alternative Grounds for Capitalism

Modern religion, science, and utilitarianism all contain defects that blunt their ability to provide what Habermas calls cultural meaning. Modern religion is so rationalized and privatized that it can exist only in the realm of subjective belief; its deistic God is too removed from ordinary experience to provide a convincing reason for being or a guide to action. (Habermas does not here address the rise of fundamentalist religions, which do not appear to have this defect.) Modern science aspires to replace religion as a source of explanation, but it unintentionally undermines itself along with its object (religion) in its attack on all dogma as mystification. Utilitarianism, finally, is unable to provide a secular foundation for ethics, for it is seen to conflict with a respect for persons.

Modern art, however, can give meaning to a capitalist existence when it is deployed as commercialized mass art. But modern art as modernistic art can also transcend this deployment and function as a subversive avant-garde. Representational (nonmodernistic) art portrayed the beautiful aspects of the social world in which it was embedded; the art of liberal capitalism said that beauty was the constant if often invisible companion (even the promise within) bourgeois society. But modernistic art jars with the conventional vision of the beautiful and presents itself as something produced rather than as the mirror of a beautiful nature and society. This art

expresses not the promise but the irretrievable sacrifice of bourgeois rationalization. . . . It strengthens the divergence between the values offered by the socio-cultural system and those demanded by the political and economic systems.[22]

The aesthetic meaning of modernistic art, says Habermas, is that capitalist society spawns a poverty of meaning.

But the most important of the attempted substitutes for privatism and tradition is norms. Premodern societies had customs that simultaneously legitimated the state and gave metaphysical meaning to life. Political and cosmological explanations were joined: there was an integral link between the "instrumental functions of administration" and the "expressive symbols that release an unspecified readiness to follow."[23] This holistic integration is precluded for advanced capitalist and all other modern states, for Enlightenment shortened the political reach of a cosmology and inaugurated the age of self-consciousness.

Within this age arose, then, the attempt to legitimate the state through self-conscious customs, that is, norms. But this attempt can issue in both a democratic state legitimated through rational discourse and a state that seeks to induce allegiance through officially manipulated belief systems. The capitalist state aims for the latter, or rather, attempts at the former are ultimately compromised by economic imperatives that demand the latter.

The capitalist state views the demise of traditional sources of meaning as an opportunity to produce norms that justify the state, but this attempt fails, says Habermas, because meaningful norms cannot be produced administratively—they must flow from a democratic discourse forbidden by capitalist priorities. A legitimating norm must "guarantee the continuity of a history through which individuals and groups can identify with themselves and with one another," but as soon as a norm is "objectively prepared and strategically employed,"[24] it loses this ability. Two examples illustrate the point. First, attempts to foster the norm "patriotism" through paid political advertisements cannot replace feelings based upon rootedness in the life of a community. They are seen instead for what they are: a manipulation of emotions that renders the emotions evoked empty. Second, the corporate slogan that without chemicals life itself would be impossible[25] intends to convey the normative message that corporate interests (the production of plastics, drugs, etc.) and the common good (life itself) coincide. But this slogan reaps only cynicism and a heightened awareness of the ways in which particular wills parade themselves as the general will.

Although the administrative production of meaning fails, nontraditional cultural meaning is possible within the terms of Habermas's ideal state, at least according to Habermas. Successful meaning-giving norms must, in modernity, meet two conditions:

First, they must speak to existential fears and doubts. Habermas's sensitivity to the human need for consolation, for "interpretations that overcome contingency," for a comforting and comfortable relation with nature, and for "intuitive access to relations of solidarity . . . between individuals"[26] displays an understanding of the attractions of holism. He is far, however, from espousing a reformulation of Faith. A return to Faith can produce cultural meaning only by appealing to elements in tradition or religion that must remain mysterious, incomplete, and partially unthematized. And this will not do, for the second condition modern norms must meet is that they be self-conscious, explicitly endorsed, rationally understood. Obviously, norms of this sort, while capable of generating cultural meaning, would be dysfunctional for capitalism—they would allow justice and capitalism to become topics of political debate.

Democratic norms in a self-conscious world (and, Habermas contends, there can be no reduction in the level of self-consciousness without repression) must express the generalizable interests of the public, the common good. These interests can be ascertained only discursively, that is, through a democratic discussion that identifies social needs and comes to a rational consensus about the norms necessary to fulfill and regulate them. Discourse for Habermas does not refer to every form of communication; it is the form whose exclusive concern is the validity of certain assertions and whose participants have agreed that only the forceless force of the better argument should prevail. In discourse "all motives except that of the cooperative search for truth are excluded."[27]

Because in every existing capitalist state the conditions necessary for a rational consensus are absent or distorted, the first step toward a legitimate, meaningful society must be a negative critique. Such a critique must be based upon a counterfactual hypothesis, a projection about which norms everyone affected would agree to without constraint if they were to enter into discourse. The key move in Habermas's argument here is that norms formed under these conditions would be rational and not simply those currently acceptable.

The requisite rationality is provided by the discursive method—it is inherent in the structure of undistorted human communication. In other words, the possibility of the rationality of norms issues from the very structure of language.

The expectation of discursive redemption of normative-validity claims is already contained in the structure of intersubjectivity. . . . In taking up a practical discourse, we unavoidably suppose an ideal speech situation that, on the strength of its formal properties, allows consensus only through *generalizable* interests.[28]

In short, the justifiability of norms is dependent upon their generalizability, that is, their ability to fulfill discursively defined common needs. The existence of a common set of needs alongside the panoply of diverse individual claims is always already guaranteed by the structure of communication. To communicate as a human is to share with all humans an interest in coming to rational agreement.

Habermas's theory of the state insists that citizens identify with the norms that govern them. It aims to close the gap between individual will and social order—in Habermas's terms to reconcile the tension between private morality and public law. The reconciliation is consensual: the products of public discourse are to be internalized as the subjective will of individuals. Habermas's theory also acknowledges that norms are conventional, but they are rationally grounded conventions. Discursively formed norms are conventional in the sense that they are conscious human artifacts but not in the sense that they are arbitrary, for they are grounded in the rationality of undistorted communication. Such norms are meaningful and form the basis of a legitimate state precisely because they are nonarbitrary conventions. Just as Enlightenment reason was believed to limit the overextension of utility, Habermas believes that discursive rationality will limit the overextension of convention.

Each of these Habermasian concepts—rationality, truth, generalizable interests, discourse, internalizable norms, and legitimacy—is an integral part of the meaning of the others. Through an understanding of these terms we uncover Habermas's ideal: the consensual state. But there is an important element within this ideal yet to be brought out—the consensual state, in order to fulfill the coordination demands made upon it, must have an instrumental view of nature.

Nature and the Technical Interest

In *Knowledge and Human Interests* Habermas argues that the view that knowledge is the objective description of the universe, the naive presumption "that the relations between empirical variables represented in theoretical propositions are self-existent," suppresses "the transcendental framework that is the precondition of the meaning of such propositions."[29] What makes knowledge possible at all (the "transcendental framework") are cognitive interests or the specific viewpoints from which humans apprehend reality. Cognitive interests

bridge the gap between the pre-scientific form of life, science and the application of scientific knowledge. "Human interests" are, in the literal sense of the word, the "inter-esse," i.e. the "being-in-between."[30]

The three cognitive interests—the technical, the practical,[31] the emancipatory[32]—stem from the fundamental conditions of human life on earth—labor, interaction, and power. I turn now to the technical interest, Habermas's defense of an instrumental view of nature.

The essence of technology is, for Habermas, domination, for the imperative of human survival requires a defensive stance toward that which poses a threat to it. "External nature" (natural forces, plants, and nonhuman animals) is a source of danger. Because humans must work on the physical environment in order to eat and reproduce, there is a built-in antagonism between humans and external nature, and humans relate to nature in part from the viewpoint of prediction and technical control. The history of technology is a history of persistent human attempts to lighten the burden of work and improve the yield from nature.

But the technical interest is more than the mere adaptation of the human organism to its environment. It is integral to the self-formative process, linked to the quest for freedom.

If we reflect on the process of self-formation, then instrumental reason, which leads to mastery over nature, and the practical reason of intersubjective communication . . . reveal themselves as integral parts of our interest in freeing ourselves from the arbitrary forces of nature and the power structures that inhibit our capacity to understand ourselves.[33]

To the holist claim that the technical interest should be subordinated to an interest in preserving and fostering the potentialities of nature, Habermas replies:

Technology . . . can only be traced back to a "project" of the human species *as a whole*, and not to one that could be historically surpassed. . . . It is impossible to envision how, as long as the organization of human nature does not change and as long therefore as we have to achieve self-preservation through social labor and with the aid of means that substitute for work, we could renounce technology, more particularly *our* technology, in favor of a qualitatively different one.[34]

Habermas endorses neither a relativist nor an objectivist conception of nature; for him nature is not a constituted object or a thing-in-itself. Although there is a sense in which nature is "an objectification of the knowing subject; . . . constituted subject to the general conditions of purposive-rational action,"[35] because the knowing subject emerges only through natural history and biological evolution, there is also a sense in which nature is the ground of subjectivity. Habermas attempts to clarify his position by differentiating between subjective nature, objective nature, and nature-in-itself.

Subjective nature is what is generally called "human nature." People have a subjective nature because they are embodied; have senses, reflexes, and instincts; and must engage in social labor. Objective nature is the earth, the physical environment, but only insofar as it exists as a complex of constituted objects, objects ready and available for use. But objective nature does not exhaust all that nature is. Evidence of the nature that remains is its resistance to false scientific interpretations. What we can know of this nature-in-itself is very little, but the glimpses we get are enough to justify positing its existence.

Nature-in-itself does not refer to unknowable but causally effective things-in-themselves; it refers instead to that moment of knowable nature designated by the terms *independence, externality, factitity*, and the like.[36]

Nature-in-itself for Habermas is a transcendental abstraction, a requisite of any knowledge of nature. Although we must presuppose this nature-in-itself, *we have access to it* (and experience its "resistance") *only in terms of its instrumentality*.

We do reckon with the existence of a reality that is independent of men who can act instrumentally and arrive at a consensus about statements. But what the predication of properties catches "of" this reality is *constituted only* in the perspective of possible technical control.[37]

Holists charge that Habermas introduces the concept "nature-in-itself" only to strip it of meaning by defining the technical interest as the one and only power of disclosing nature. Habermas describes the criticism: "My specifications of instrumental and communicative rationality are drawn too narrowly to permit an adequate distinction between external nature as a means for us and nature as an end-in-itself."[38] Habermas then admits to this and other criticisms: his distinction between subjective nature, objective nature, and nature-in-itself has not sufficiently clarified the relation between reason and nature, for it is difficult to see how a nature-in-itself that is an "abstracton" can also be a natural process that grounds the subjectivity of the natural being man; he has not provided a good account of how one might relate from a nonobjectivist perspective to a "thick" notion of nature-in-itself. Habermas argues, however, that these problems stem not from any particular weakness in the theory of cognitive interests but from limitations in human knowledge per se. He attempts, then, to provide an epistemological defense of an instrumental view of nature. And the view that nature is knowable only from the viewpoint of possible technical control is, moreover, the only position compatible with a disenchanted view of nature.

Although it is possible to experience nature as a nonobjectified environment, these rapturous experiences must take the form of art, transcendental meditation, or unarticulated stirring within the soul. In short, "the phenomena that are exemplary for a moral-practical, 'fraternal,' relation to nature are most unclear, if one does not want to have recourse . . . to mystically inspired philosophies of nature."[39] Any theoretically fruitful theory of knowledge cannot base itself on these nonrational stirrings. Habermas refuses to underplay the success of modern science in explaining the natural world and is not now about to abandon its model in the study of "the relation between reason and nature." (For Habermas, humans are so defined by their rational subjectivity that "reason" can take their place in this relation.) The only theoretical alternative to a reenchanted philosophy of nature is Habermas's: the relation between reason and nature must be conceived instrumentally, and nature can have, at most, only a moment of in-itselfness.

If at the level of a theory of knowledge only an objectifying conception of nature is possible, can an environmental ethic be had where nature-in-itself emerges? Habermas says no, arguing that any ethic must consider only interpersonal relations, that is, must be a "discourse ethic." Intuitively, the attempt to open up a moral path to nature-in-itself is not absurd, "but we should not permit ourselves to be cajoled by these intuitions into ignoring the difficulties that we encounter [in the attempt]."[40] What are these difficulties?

First, basic ethical concepts like justice, equality, and freedom rely on a type of relation that can arise only between human subjects engaged in discourse, and this "in principle egalitarian relation of reciprocity . . . cannot be carried over into the relation between humans and nature in any strict sense."[41] Participants in ethical relations must by definition have the capacity for autonomy and responsibility; nature-in-itself may have elements of the former but certainly not the latter.

Second, a nonanthropocentric ethic cannot mediate between the human need to draw sustenance from nature and the obligation to respect it in itself. How is it possible, for example, to have sympathetic solidarity with plants that one must eat?

In sum, the distinction between subjective nature, objective nature, and nature-in-itself allows Habermas to argue that a noninstrumental view of nature cannot be "adequately grounded today without recourse to the substantial reason of religion or metaphysical worldviews."[42] The attempt to retrieve the lost unity of life and to abolish thereby the distinction between the technical, practical, and emancipatory interests cannot succeed. The best his anti-Promethean critics can offer, says Habermas, is a nostalgic appeal to a distant pastoral scene.

The second key distinction in his defense of an instrumental view of nature, that between work and interaction, is a response to the charge that the domination of nature fosters the domination of humans—the charge made by natural holists against environmental managers. The work-interaction distinction also allows Habermas to discuss the way technology today functions to legitimate capitalism; he thus ties his philosophy of nature to the theory of legitimation crisis.

Work, says Habermas, is the sphere of instrumental, purposive-rational action, governed by technical rules, based on empirical knowledge. Interaction is the sphere of communicative, institution-maintaining action, governed by consensual norms, based in ordinary language. Habermas believes that domination is ineliminable in the relation between reason and nature—that is, in the sphere of work—and thus concentrates his emancipatory efforts within the sphere of interaction. Indeed, the domination in the sphere of interaction—political repression, inequality, injustice—is the product of an illegitimate extension of the technical interest. Because instrumentality cannot be eradicated from the human condition, and because domination clearly exists in social interactions, the boundary between work and interaction must have been violated in modernity. Habermas seeks then to fortify or "rationalize" the sphere of interaction, but whereas the rationalization of work would entail an extension of technical control, the rationalization of interaction demands the extension of communication free from domination.[43]

The technical interest has infiltrated into the practical and emancipatory ones because it has taken on a new, legitimating function for the advanced capitalist state. In traditional societies technically exploitable knowledge did not threaten the authority of cultural or religious traditions that legitimated political power; in the capitalist state technology and science are called upon to legitimate a state whose main role has become the guarantor of efficient production. Although the forces of production once (in liberal capitalism) functioned to spur changes in outmoded social institutions, technology now serves more as an ideological justification of the state than as a critique of state ideologies. The legitimation of technocracy by technology depoliticizes a process that ought to be, in a democratic state, the province of communicative, normative action.

Habermas, Lowi, and the Enlightenment Inheritance

Although Lowi shares with Habermas an instrumental view of nature, it is clear that the consensual ideal is also a critique of Lowi's theory of the state: Lowi's espousal of neo-laissez-faire displays a naiveté about the economic imperatives of advanced capitalism; Lowi does not delve deeply enough into the question of legitimacy, which he misidentifies as a mere matter of defective administration.

But both Lowi and Habermas thematize the discord between the democratic rhetoric of modern Western states and their actual practices. Lowi exposes corporate influence on public policy, an influence that procedural democracy may reform; Habermas offers a complex, systemic critique of capitalism and a collectivist alternative. Lowi defines the central problem of the state as the tension between bureaucratic power and bargaining on the rule (what Habermas would see as a crippled version of discursive will-formation); a high degree of administrative discretion is at odds with a commitment to representative democracy. Habermas conceives the problem in terms of a tension between capitalism and legitimacy; a capitalist state must legitimate itself as democratic *and* obscure an unjust class compromise. For Habermas, administrative discretion is not a problem for the capitalist state; it is, rather, an integral part of a system that seeks to minimize occasions for system-questioning public discourse. And Lowi's solution to administrative discretion—juridical polity, neo-laissez-faire economy—also serves this aim.

Legitimation Crisis is an account of this dilemma: a modern state must extend the reach of public policy, but a modern capitalist state can fulfill this coordination task only at the expense of cultural meaning. It shows, first, that the capitalist state requires more legitimacy than it can muster and, second, that the missing legitimacy *could* be supplied (through consensual norms) with no sacrifice of coordination power—that is, with no reduction in the areas of life requiring public organization and control. Like Lowi, Habermas does not thematize the need to relax the drive for social coordination and economic mastery.

The extension of public policy is a requirement of any viable modern state with a self-conscious citizenry, says Habermas. As the homogenization of consumer items, the increased sophistication of communication systems, and population growth make the world smaller and more interdependent, new responsibilities arise for the state: the coordination of food supplies, distribution of education and training, and the prevention of (preparation for) nuclear war. Moreover, the modern state can rely only tenuously on the organizational powers of religion, myth, or tradition. Habermas believes it crucial that equally powerful substitutes be found. Whereas the capitalist state substitutes technocratic and commercially controlled policy for these decayed forces, the Habermasian state would substitute consensual, rational, and internalized norms. Like Lowi, Habermas believes that a state capable of extensive planning is a positive good; it enables freedom, where freedom is the ability to exercise self-assertion in a world ordered (individually according to Lowi, and collectively according to Habermas) by humans.

"Standard" critiques of Habermas take this view of freedom for granted, focusing on the difficulties he has in bringing his quest for a legitimate state in tune with his theory of communication. The ideal speech situation, they say, is to ground the rational consensual state—but if Habermas's quasi-transcendental argument should falter, his state would lose its prospective ability to spawn cultural meaning, and it would thereby lose the ability to ensure its own legitimacy. These critics ask not whether the extensive coordination imperatives of the modern state could be relaxed but whether a set of consensual norms can be identified with the reach and power necessary to the extensive coordination imperatives of the modern state. In order to differentiate these two questions, I will give a brief account of the standard critique of Habermas and then turn to a critique wary of the equation between freedom and mastery.

According to an early critique, the key flaw in Habermas's consensual ideal is his inability to distinguish between norms that express generalizable interests and those that express exclusive interests. Desiring a democratic state, yet fearful of a link between a consensual state and a fascist one, these critics wondered about the relativism within Habermas's theory. Does not the viability of norms depend upon an essentially arbitrary "*decision* whether or not to let one's actions be guided only by maxims" in tune with the common good?[44]

Habermas's response to this was to move to the metatheoretical level in order to find a rational grounding for norms; his answer was the consensus theory of truth. This theory then became the new focus of attack: it "understates the extent to which our limited resources of reason and evidence unavoidably generate a plurality of reasonable answers to perplexing practical questions."[45] Habermas, according to this critique, develops a subtle and complex notion of rationality that acknowledges, especially when pressed by hermeneuticists, reason's inevitable blind spots, but he does not seem to recognize the implications of this essentially limited reason for a politics of discursive will-formation.[46]

Habermas then responded to this charge with two claims: rational consensus is an ever-elusive, perpetually postponed achievement, a guiding ideal; and the ideal speech situation functions only as proof of the theoretical possibility of consensus. But these claims still left his theory open to the charge of repressive utopianism—utopian in that it is an unattainable ideal, repressive in that the attempt to attain it requires coercion.[47] Yes, the ideal speech situation is the exception rather than the rule and "not all interactions fall into the category of action orientated to reaching understanding";[48] granted, "negotiated . . . agreements based on the intersubjective necessity of criticisable validity-claims are diffuse, fleeting . . . and fragile"[49]—but more serious indeed is the fact that Habermas's own qualification of the scope of communicative action reacts disruptively on the theory of the state that provided the initial need for a theory of communicative action. The state is not merely a symbolic locus of intersubjectivity; as Habermas himself insists, it is a powerful actor in the world.

An anti-Promethean perspective on the state exempts itself from these debates about the ideal speech situation or the significance of Habermas's move to the metatheoretical level. Regardless of whether rational consensus is possible, it asks whether it is desirable. It focuses upon the ways in which the very quest for consensus is destructive, with how it excludes or distorts aspects of life that cannot be expressed according to the standards of rational discourse.

This critique begins by recalling a defect in Enlightenment: the faith in the automatic ability of reason to limit the overextension of utility was shown to be unwarranted as world and self became increasingly subject to the standards of instrumental rationality. This faith, however, still finds expression in Habermas's assumption that a fully normative and normalized social order would be a free society.

By focusing upon a critique of capitalism, Habermas's theory of the state distances itself from liberal theories such as Lowi's, but at a level deeper than the economic organization of the state it shares much with them. In the most general terms, Habermas and Lowi share a great esteem for human subjects around whom the world must be made to fit. Reason is the primary tool for this tailoring job: reason applied to will and impulse must discipline inner nature or the instinctual, chaotic self; reason transformed into social science and public policy must forge a social order; reason as physical science and technology must subdue outer nature or the environment; reason applied to collective will must deploy these rationalized materials in pursuit of the common good. Reason, freedom, and mastery thus become terms that engender and sustain each other in the underlying system of thought guiding each theory.

Habermas's ideal has exposed oppressive potentialities of Lowi's state: Lowi's restriction of the state to administrative and procedural functions made it too weak to realize the public interest it promised, and neo-laissez-faire would simply empower the corporate structure to set the moral and political agenda for the nation. Lowi's attempt to strengthen the legal powers at the state's disposal, in the absence of a critique of capitalist production, serves only to highlight and publicize the need (for the sake of the stability of the order) to organize life around the imperatives of corporate capitalism and to specify in detail the punitive measures necessary to fulfill them.

Habermas's discursive will-formation would be less likely to legitimate corporate imperatives, for the corporate system is itself called into question. A Habermasian state might be able to resist economistic priorities, but it is a state so strong and so implicated in social life that it has oppressive potentialities of its own. The discursive state, encouraged to be active and powerful for the sake of its role as locus of collective freedom, also courts authoritarianism. Lowi's commitment to mastery took the form of an obsession with a predictable, precise, and legalized social order that left only some economic decisions unregulated; Habermas's commitment to mastery takes the form of a relentlessly rational, norm-governed state that would leave even less of life untouched—one is hard pressed to find areas protected from discursive thematization. Habermas's ideal state threatens to colonize every refuge for protest against rationalization.

Habermas is not unaware of this danger. He anticipates the criticism that when thematized norms cover an extensive slice of life, unorthodox ideas are imperiled by the social tendency to accept as given "the interpretation of needs . . . current at any . . . contingent stage of socialization."[50] Habermas responds to this danger by distinguishing between norm and principle (a metanorm from which norms can be generated).

Internalization . . . would only be complete when the principle of the justification of possible principles (that is, the readiness to engage in discursive clarification of practical questions) was alone internalized, but in other respects the continuous interpretation of needs was given over to communication processes.[51]

In other words, the Habermasian state seeks an unquestioning commitment to the *principle* of rational discussion, a principle that precludes an unquestioning acceptance of any particular *norm*. Citizens will have thoroughly internalized the principle of rational discourse, but their views as to the particular content of a norm must wait until the communication process has taken place. Norms are contingent conventions rightly subjected to constant reevaluation on the basis of a necessary commitment to the principle of rational discourse; in this way, norms are not internalized to the extent that critical thought or social change is precluded.

Still, claims the anti-Promethean critique, criticism and change are judged entirely by a standard of what norms are rational in a highly integrated and coordinated society. There is little attentiveness to the limits of rational mastery, and from an anti-Promethean perspective, rational mastery of social life is a Sisyphean task. Blind to its futility, however, the Habermasian social project seriously endangers cultural protest, and the Habermasian conception of nature imperils the very foundation of biological life.

The discussions of the ideal states of Lowi and Habermas and of their flaws have prepared the way for an account of the anti-Promethean theory of the state.

The Attuned State

In the conclusion to his book on Hegel, Charles Taylor asks why Hegel's thought has retained its importance while the Hegelian ontology has been abandoned. Taylor's answer is, in essence, that Hegel's identification of the structure of modern thought was basically correct even if his philosophy could not transcend it. It is fitting, then, that the last theorist of the state to be considered here is Taylor, for his thought is self-consciously defined by the Faith-Enlightenment framework. And if one draws out Taylor's theory of the state, one sees that it too has a Hegelian ring: the subject of the *Phenomenology*, who comes to recognize *Geist*, becomes Taylor's embodied self, properly attuned to its world. Taylor brings Hegel into the modern age.

Taylor translates Hegel's dialectic into a contemporary vocabulary, arguing that there are two conflicting strands of modern thought. The first responds to the disenchantment of nature with a faith that technical control can resecure the world. We have already spoken of this in terms of the Promethean urge. The other strand Taylor calls expressivist. It too faces disenchantment but is critical of the Promethean ideal where "all our acts, objects, institutions have a use, but none expresses what men are or could be."[52] The voice of expressivism today is protest—unable to present itself as the voice of an authentic but violated nature, it can object, for the sake of an authentic but violated *self*, to the predictable, homogenized, rationalized world the Promethean seeks to install.

If the historical experience of objectifying and transforming nature . . . is too powerful for it to survive as an interlocutor; then the expressivist current of opposition to modern civilization has to focus on man.[53]

But the "focus on man" carries with it a danger that expressivism will become what it protests against—a masterful, anthropocentric orientation. Taylor seeks to avoid this by endorsing an expressivism where attunement with the world, rather than its mastery, is the precondition of self-realization. His ideal state is founded on this same principle of attunement.

I will first provide an account of the steady-state economy endorsed by Taylor; I then explore his critique of Promethean socialism, a theory that claims to reject utilitarianism while endorsing an instrumental view of nature; finally, I consider the philosophical anthropology that guides his theory of the state, an attuned expressivism.

The Steady State

In "The Politics of the Steady State" Taylor rejects the pursuit of economic growth and rejects the vision of the good life that requires "an ever-increasing command over goods and services and an ever-increasing capacity to control nature for individual ends."[54] Instead, the steady state is to build an economy of recycling technologies and moderate consumption levels, where the normal pattern of consumption is accessible to the least affluent. While there can be minor deviations from the norm, the possessions a normal, decent life requires would be universally distributed. This universal consumption standard need not be a colorless world of utility goods, for once we have abandoned the equation of consumption with happiness, it should be possible "for people to elaborate new and original ways of living in balance with nature"[55] and to express their creativity in ways other than the proliferation of consumer items.

A universal consumption standard contrasts sharply with the orientation to consumption fostered within an economy of growth. The logic there says, "More is better, freer, easier, happier." But in order to evaluate whether one is getting more, one compares not only what one has now to what one had last year but also what one has relative to others. Once a society has provided for the essential material needs of its citizens, which the advanced industrial nations for the most part have, the pursuit of further economic growth, because of the pressures to maintain the existing structures of employment, corporate power, and international relations, places a higher and higher premium on exclusive goods—goods valued precisely because few others have them, goods whose enjoyability decreases as they are made more widely available. The private automobile is an example of an exclusive good (its speed, efficiency, and convenience decrease as traffic increases).

The relative deprivation factor in the assessment of one's achievement of the good life as socially defined helps to explain why individual economic advance in an economy of growth is experienced as disappointing even as it remains a compelling goal. If one doubles one's consumption level while others already ahead on the income ladder do likewise, the increase in freedom will be less than anticipated: "The ever-increasing expectations of consumers outrun the rise in production with relative ease, and there is probably more resentment today . . . than . . . a few years ago."[56] An economy of growth makes the good life elusive except for those at the very top of the consumption hierarchy. Although this relative deprivation factor operates in all societies, a society in pursuit of exponential growth, by defining the good life so heavily in terms of consumption, exacerbates its socially divisive effect.

Many of the flaws in the existing state that the steady state is designed to redress—the power of large corporations, the priority of exclusive goods, the reduction of freedom to the choice among things or candidates for consumption—are also identified as flaws from within a collectivist perspective. For both the steady statist and the collectivist, the way to displace these orientations and institutions is through collective effort; so Taylor shares some of Habermas's faith in the ability of self-conscious agents to foster social change.

The universal consumption standard, for example, would require conscious public control of economic production; those consumption items necessary to a decent life and within the limits of environmental toleration would be established politically and then enforced through a systematic policy of rationing and subsidies.

The goods of the standard would be available to everyone's budget, but . . . the goods and services outside this range, being relatively starved of resources and unsubsidized, would be much more highly priced.[57]

The problem for Taylor at this point is that a state strong enough to shape the modern economy is also a state susceptible to the abuse of political power, especially as it finds expression in the overregulation of its populace or the subjection of more and more areas of life to bureaucratic regulation. The paradox of political freedom rears its ugly head even for Taylor.

Acknowledging that conscious coordination of the economy is a form of power, Taylor diffuses this dangerous power by making coordination a function of deeply felt norms rather than officially imposed regulations. Citizens internalize steady-state norms, incorporating them into personal identity. These norms are, moreover, understood as more than social conveniences or rational conventions; norms are necessary, given that individual identity cannot exist outside of a social order. Norms limit individual behavior as they help constitute identity; norms are a requirement of being human. Good norms, norms worthy of endorsement, are those that help to foster a wholesome identity by allowing expression of individualism even as they remind one of one's cultural debt. Taylor's emphasis on the social dimension of personal identity means that a steady state must be grounded in the reflective allegiance of its citizens, even if the attuned state does not require allegiance to be as explicit and self-conscious as it must be in Habermas's state.

Although a political economy of growth also allows a particular sense of self to emerge (citizens identify themselves as self-dependent beings who shape nature to freely chosen projects and who are entitled to prosperity), this understanding of self is, for Taylor, narrow and alienating. In contrast, a steady state encourages citizens to see their identity, their goals, and their fulfillment as essentially tied to a larger whole.

How does one begin to replace a social identity of economic growth with one where "we accept, and hence come to value, a balance of some kind with our surroundings,"[58] where we have "a very strong sense of common purpose,"[59] and where we "respond to the end of growth . . . as a challenging common task which binds [and not as] . . . a disaster in which each must scramble for safety on his own"?[60] The attuned state requires a vast amount of civic virtue, and is thus embroiled in the classic dilemma identified by Rousseau: to foster a social identity of civic virtue one requires beforehand the very condition that is sought. While Taylor is by no means confident that this dilemma can be overcome, he does not rule out the following optimistic scenario (most likely to emerge in "small societies or societies which can be meaningfully decentralized"):[61]

The initial transition to a radically equalized consumption level is imposed by a resource or population crisis. Then, through "a kind of Dunkirk spirit,"[62] we weather the storm with free institutions intact and a universal consumption standard tentatively in place. The very experience of a universal consumption standard might then evoke the civic virtue necessary to its institutional and psychological perpetuation and refinement.

"The Politics of the Steady State" is the most explicit statement of the political economy of the attuned state, but it alludes only darkly to the philosophical convictions that ground it. I move now to Taylor's discussion of socialism, for his critique of its Promethean dimension clarifies these convictions.

Promethean Socialism

The humanist Marxist has protested against our "wretchedly contented" civilization, which makes fetishes out of commodities and alienated workers out of human beings. He has been a witness for the possibility of a life where the instrumental and the expressive dimensions of activities are joined, thus permitting a reintegrated human personality. But the reconciliation of the strategic self with the creative self necessitates a bigger reunion—individuals must come to see themselves as integrally connected to a larger world; they must feel at home in the world. Self-fulfillment requires attunement to that elusive thing called human nature, identification with available social roles, and solidarity with the natural environment.

But this socialist ideal, says Taylor, seeks to situate humans in the larger scheme of things by *humanizing* the larger scheme, and therein lies its Promethean cast. Human aims, as they are expressed in individual personalities and social roles, are to be "reconciled" with natural processes and events by making nature conform to human aims. Harmony with nature is achieved through remolding it. Promethean transformation of the world becomes the solution to the expressive deadness of the modern age.

Transformation is not exactly mastery, for it requires a more subtle relationship of subject to object: the human personality must invest itself creatively in the object to be transformed, and it usually does this through labor, as a woodworker transforms a tree into a table. To master a tree, on the other hand, is to raze it, dig up its roots, and pave over the soil—to eradicate all traces rather than to reconstitute form. But transformation and mastery have this in com-mon: neither adequately appreciates the integrity of that which is to be reformed according to a conscious, human design.

And this transformation of nature, says Taylor, cannot take the socialist where he wants to go. Transformation of nature, initially a requirement of self-fulfillment, ultimately entails a science of self as well as a natural science. The socialist ideal requires that we transform inner nature as well as outer nature: for if our instinctual, passionate selves are not brought into line, society will be too con-tentious, fractious, and volatile to be a home. But to do that which would be necessary to control and homogenize self and society would be to erase the expressive, the creative, the unpredictable, the innovative. Taylor concludes that the socialist "reconciliation" of the instrumental and the expressive strands degenerates once again into the triumph of instrumental rationality.

For example, although Habermas has certainly tried, he has not come up with a convincing way to confine the Promethean orien-tation to nonhuman nature. Says Taylor, while "the example of the sculptor certainly shows that man can have both an expressive and an objectifying relation to nature at once"[63]—the clay is trans-formed through the imposition of creative will and the sculptor realizes herself in the imposition—humans are not clay, and so-cialism is a social theory not an individual's aesthetic project. A populace rationalized according to a "science of man in society which identifies the determinants of people's behavior" is a popu-lace where "some men are controlling or manipulating others."[64] Thus, the expressive dimension of Habermas's theory is still always in danger of being swallowed up by the instrumental; his distinction between the technical interest on the one hand and the practical and emancipatory interests on the other cannot save him.

The socialist commitment to self-realization is real, but it releases human creativity from the bounds of utilitarian work and instru-mental thought at the price of a conception of nature as standing reserve. Although this is a price the socialist may be willing to pay, given the greater good of opportunities for self-expression through transformation of nature, the objectifying orientation to nature will ultimately objectify the self. Socialist expressivism, says Taylor, endangers the environment and cannot prevent the danger from spreading to humans.

While the proposals of Taylor's steady state have significant elements in common with Habermas's state, it is this Promethean element he seeks to correct. Taylor strives to articulate an expressivism that can foster self-realization and a certain sensitivity to the natural bent of things. The manipulation of nature that governs the Habermasian ideal gives way to a quest for attunement to nature.

A second difficulty Taylor has with socialism is its view of freedom. Freedom is the ability to assert one's will and express one's self through transformation of nature. This freedom is situationless, requiring release from the constraints of the world; "to be free is to be untrammeled, to depend in one's actions only on oneself,"[65] for only then can alienation be overcome. But this self-dependent self-assertion is not a sufficient conception of freedom, even in socialist terms, says Taylor. It neatly captures the dimension of freedom relevant to isolated individuals, but it fails to consider the political dimension of freedom. And socialist freedom aspires to collective self-expression, which requires dialogue, political discourse—more than the technical proficiency of labor or craftsmanship.

Socialist freedom, in order to fulfill its own collectivist aims, must come to grips with the limits to sociality, to human communication, to a rational society. Even if some socialists acknowledge the masterful, rational state to be only an ideal, even theoretical accommodation to limits is fundamentally at odds with a Promethean orientation to nature. The pursuit of a situationless freedom, says Taylor with Hegel,[66] will ultimately compromise concern for a state with which citizens can collectively identify.

Taylor insists that freedom be situated. But what is the "situation" that "sets goals for us . . . imparts a shape to rationality and provides an inspiration for creativity"?[67] To explore what Taylor means by "situation" is to give content to his claim that there is a natural bent in self and nature to which it is politically possible to be attuned.

Attuned Expressivism

For Taylor a human being is not a composite of disparate "faculties" or an uneasy compound of body and soul but a unified, coherent whole. It has properties and functions proper and internal to it and properties and pseudo-functions alien and external to it. If one understands the holistic structure of the self a telos in the object of inquiry will emerge, a natural tendency toward certain modes of being. To understand holistically, rather than atomistically, is to be able to discern an authentic self beneath each particular cultural expression of it. Taylor is sympathetic to the socialist project insofar as it too understands that a way of life, a political economy, can either enable or distort what we authentically are.[68] A true expressivist will seek to expose even hidden channels of social access to individual identity in order to discern whether the self is being realized or thwarted by roles, institutions, customs, or laws.

An authentic existence is in tune with the bent of humanness; it assents to the grain of personhood.

Our identity is . . . defined by certain evaluations which are inseparable from ourselves as agents. Shorn of these we would cease to be ourselves, by which we do not mean trivially that we would be different in the sense of having some properties other than those we now have . . .—but that . . . we would lose the very possibility of . . . our existence as persons.[69]

What are these "certain evaluations" that constitute personhood? Taylor has in mind a specific set of conceptual distinctions and normative pursuits ineliminable to human beings; his argument is not simply that some set (any old set) of culturally variable categories of understanding are essential to a meaningful human life. Taylor's "certain evaluations" include the ability to distinguish between "noble" and "base"; the capacity for responsibility, agency, reflection; and the pursuit of integrity (an integrated personality) and dignity. In his critique of situationless freedom, too, the societal "situation" required to realize the common good was not arbitrary but linked to Taylor's quite specific notion of the highest human good.

Who is the "we" whose identity depends upon these "certain eval-uations"? The "we" seems to slide among (1) "we who self-con-sciously distinguish between noble and base, who seek to become responsible, reflective, unified and dignified agents," (2) "we who are responsible agents by habit or convention," (3) "we who are unwilling heirs of our historical situation," (4) "we who are mod-ern humans," and (5) "we who are humans."

These are not exactly slides, for there is a way in which all of the "we's" coincide for Taylor—humans as such (#5) are more authen-tic the closer they approach #1 on the scale, the more they under-stand themselves to be what they are already becoming: reflective, expressive evaluators.

An important second feature of Taylor's discussion of "situation" is the role articulation (or, more broadly, language) plays in human identity.

Language, given by one's cultural situation, enables human iden-tity by providing a shared background of concepts and terms with which to communicate. But it also limits, for we can never be the masters of this rich and deep thing called language. In his discussion of the self, Taylor develops his position primarily through a contrast with atomism; in his discussion of the role language plays in human identity his opponent is the designative theory of language.

> Language is not an assemblage of separable instruments . . . which can be used to marshall ideas, this use being something we can fully control and oversee. Rather it is . . . a web. . . . Because the words we use now only have a sense through their place in the whole web, we can never in prin-ciple have a clear oversight of the implications of what we say. . . . Our language is always more than we can encompass.[70]

The inexhaustibility of language stems both from its historical density and from the finitude of the individual self. Language ex-presses. But what does it express? The first answer is the self, or rather the highest, most authentic human self, for the optimal self clarifies and thus brings into being different human feelings or ex-periences. It is a self that can discern, upon reflection, the subtle differences between embarrassment and annoyance or fatigue and discouragement or apprehension and anxiety. The second answer is the world, for in expressing/realizing our selves we are at the same time "responding to the reality in which we are set, in which we are included, of course, but which is not reducible to our experience of it."[71] By including the second answer, Taylor attempts to correct for the anthropocentrism of the socialist attempt at expressivism.

When we use language to interpret an event or to make a moral evaluation, we express neither subjective preferences nor objective descriptions. Rather, articulations "are attempts to formulate what is initially inchoate, or confused. . . . This kind of formulation . . . doesn't leave its object unchanged."[72] But neither does it wholly constitute it. That "initially inchoate" stuff is what we seek to attune ourselves *to*. One clear thing Taylor can say, then, about "the bent of things" is that humans help bring it into being by articulating it. We real-ize it by recognizing it in words.

This view of language whereby humans are specially interpreters of the world resonates of the view of the world as a divine text. Language doesn't simply refer to something it then "represents"; rather, it manifests something, a something that can be called being. "There is a distinction between distorted and authentic self-understanding. . . . The latter can in a sense be said to follow a direction in being."[73]

"Situation" then has not only a human facet, that is, what is required for human identity and by an intersubjective linguistic community, but also a nonhuman facet, that is, what is required by "the world," or "reality." We can evaluate Taylor's claim that there is superindividual and supercultural "direction in being" by examining his view of natural science.

Taylor acknowledges with Kuhn and others that interpretation is involved in natural science, that all natural science explanations rest upon a background of prescientific understandings about the physical universe, what it is, and how it exists. Still, claims Taylor, that is not to say that reality is subjective or even intersubjective. "It has seemed a sound principle of scientific explanation since the seventeenth century that the world should be accounted for in ab-solute terms,"[74] that is, terms not dependent upon the meanings the world has for humans. For Taylor, natural science "really illumi-nates the natural universe."[75]

The reason the Galileo-Descartes model of science triumphed over the world-as-text model, says Taylor, is because the former fit the universe better.

It might have been the case that the theories of the high Renaissance . . . would have turned out to be better science . . . but that would have been because the way in which things react and relate to each other would have been of the kind which is characterizable in the concepts of correspondence, meaning, and so on. The universe would have been very different.[76]

Human powers of perception are better in tune with the universe when they employ the Descartes-Galileo model of science. Evidence of this is that it works better. Attunement between science and nature is not a product of convention for Taylor—modern science did not triumph simply because the scientific community came to a consensus about it. Rather, nature allows and disallows a range of scientific interpretations. There is a primordial, albeit murky, connection between the world and us, between the world and the appearance given to us.

Although Taylor rejects a purely objective social science, where the social scientist seeks a language that segregates "reality" from "experience," he understands its appeal. "Absolute description . . . seems to offer the hope of intersubjective agreement free from interpretive dispute."[77] Objectivism is one way to avoid relativism in social theory; Taylor offers an expressivism of attunement as another.

The plausibility of Taylor's steady-state ideal depends upon the plausibility of the philosophical anthropology that underpins it, and this expressivism of attunement has had to convince on several fronts:

First, it had to show that any meaningful human existence requires a "situation": a culture, a language, a natural environment, an inherent capacity for "certain evaluations."

Second, it had to show that this "horizon of the implicit, of unreflected life and experience"[78] is not fully amenable to human manipulation (but resists some human actions and interpretations and is amenable to others), but nevertheless is one to which we belong.

He must articulate a "situation" with which we can be attuned but with which we never coincide; he must describe "a freedom rooted in our nature, and yet which can be frustrated by our own desires."[79] Taylor attempted to do this through a holism that putatively exhibits a telos in the self and through an appeal to the superior explanatory power of modern science.

Third, Taylor must convince us that the best way to relate to such a world is to make ourselves consonant with it. Taylor's strategy for this task is the extensive and repeated use of suggestive metaphors. Taylor tells us that we really should seek

- "a deep endorsement of the course of things"[80]
- "an affirmation of this defining situation as ours"[81]
- "the notion of a bent in our situation which we can either endorse or reject, re-interpret or distort"[82]
- "a conception of man in which free action is the response to what we are—or to a call which comes to us."[83]

It is my contention that although Taylor has some success with the first two tasks, he fails with the last. But that is the one in which he must succeed to vindicate his theory.

A Critique of the Attuned State

On the one hand, Taylor's formulations strive to evoke the resistance or moment of otherness of the world. He wants to retain an absolutist moment in natural science because there must be a world "out there" in some sense that we can be attuned *to*. So when some philosophers of science dissolve the world into intersubjectivity, Taylor is concerned to preserve the moment of truth in the objectivist view of science: natural objects, Taylor insists, are independent enough to resist or stimulate us. Thus, when Taylor speaks of "the appearance given to the world,"[84] he offers a carefully crafted phrase. He does not say "the appearance of the world," for that could imply the existence of a full-fledged independent "reality" behind the "appearance." Nor does he say "the appearance we give to the world," for that could imply that we create the world ex nihilo and the world is but the "appearance" we give to it. To say instead that there is an "appearance given to the world" is to suggest that although we participate in the making of the world (the world becomes more "real" as it appears to us in perception, as we interpret it, live it), the world is also already there, given to us with a peculiar appearance, presented to us with a specific face.

On the other hand, Taylor believes that this recalcitrant nature need not remain alien, for it is in truth an amicable companion for humans if only we give it its due, acknowledge it, and respect it in our interactions with it. Ultimately, an attuned orientation to the world can enable us to "straddle the gap between things and our experience of them."[85]

Here we see what a fine line Taylor must walk. He is concerned to defend a moment of resistance in nature, a moment indicative of the presence of an inherent order in nature, but his assumption that we can harmonize ourselves with this order without much violence done to ourselves or nature makes the already-quasi independence of nature weaker and weaker. Taylor's expressivism, exemplified by the phrase "the appearance given to the world," implies two incompatible claims: (1) the world is other to us, partly opaque, and (2) the world is accessible and can be in harmony with us.

This tension is neither resolved nor further refined by Taylor. He convinces us that the world is never transparent to us, but when we ask why the correct response to this murky world is attunement, he cannot provide a definitive answer that would rule out all other orientations to the world. It is crucial for his theory of the state that Taylor supply such an answer, otherwise the attuned steady state cannot generate the civic virtue necessary to it.

Why ought we pursue an expressive project of harmonization? Why do we "need" notions like a natural bent to the world? And what in the world speaks to that need? Taylor's answer seems to be that harmonization is superior because all other modern orientations have serious problems. Taylor argues by elimination:

(1) The unconscious unity of self and nature of Robust Faith is

impossible once the level of self-consciousness passes a certain point in its historical development.

(2) The instrumental, utilitarian orientation of Enlightenment destroys nature and leaves humans alienated and open to manipulation.

(3) The pursuit of an unsituated, self-dependent existence through Promethean transformation of nature reduces to 2 and has authoritarian tendencies.

For Taylor, only one approach left holds the promise of an authentic existence: we will be most free if we acknowledge our situatedness and attempt to harmonize ourselves with it. The same structure of persuasion applies to all of Taylor's essays, whether they address the question of the best ethical theory, the ideal state, the most defensible concept of the person, the relation of language to being, or the structure of the natural sciences.[86] Taylor's critique of alternative approaches to these topics evokes our sense of their inadequacy and suggests or implies that an orientation of attunement is the only viable path open.

But, even if Taylor did destroy all possible opponents, the argument by elimination would not necessarily establish Taylor's position. It could be that the opponents foster faulty understandings of freedom and politics even while Taylor's alternative in incapable of realization. Perhaps Taylor's expressivism expresses a longing rather than a real possibility.

Perhaps the persistent urge in the self to be at one with nature, the longing to believe that the world has an inherent structure with which we can be in harmony and which can bring to fruition an authentic human life, does not imply anything but an unfulfillable human need. Perhaps it does not mean that there exists a natural bent in the self or in the universe that can satisfy it.

Taylor first established a moment of objectivity, a bent, in the self and the universe in order that there be something non-subject-derived to guide subjects. But that nonsubjective something, while difficult to deny, may be incapable of the degree of guidance "attunement" implies; it might be discernible by reason or emotion only sporadically and too weak or confusing to unify human being.

There is, as Taylor himself admits, a "gap between things and our experience of them," but that gap is not necessarily the exclusive product of nonattuned orientations like utilitarianism.

Promethean theories of the state deny the integrity of nature and the resistance of self and society to rational order. They are like lions devouring their prey. The attuned state is also unable, finally, to consider the potential extent of that resistance. It is like an amoeba suffocating its victim, killing it by incorporating it into a larger "unity." In the theory of the attuned state, faith in a natural telos has moved from belief in a divinely inspired nature to belief in the possibility of an authentic reconciliation of self and nature.

A dubious theory of attunement underlies Taylor's steady state. Is there a theory of the state that neither gives free rein to the Promethean urge nor seeks to incorporate the world into higher and higher levels of rationality? Chapter 4 is directed to this inquiry.

NOTES

1. Paul Ricoeur, "The Paradox of Politics," in *Legitimacy and the State*, ed. William Connolly (Oxford: Basil Blackwell, 1984), p. 261.

2. William E. Connolly, *Appearance and Reality in Politics* (Cambridge: Cambridge University Press, 1981), pp. 165–66.

3. Theodore J. Lowi, *The End of Liberalism*, 2nd ed. (New York: W. W. Norton, 1979), p. 276.

4. Lowi, p. 296.

5. Lowi, p. 311.

6. Lowi, p. 307.

7. Lowi, p. 305.

8. Lowi, p. 298.

9. Lowi, p. 312.

10. Lowi, p. 289.

11. Lowi, p. 285.

12. Lowi, p. 291.

13. Lowi, p. 292.

14. Lowi, p. 292.

15. Lowi, p. 293.

16. Lowi, p. 293.

17. Lowi, p. 293.

18. For example: Education curriculum, city development, health, family and sexual relations.

19. Jürgen Habermas, *Legitimation Crisis* (Boston: Beacon, 1973), p. 78.

20. Habermas, *Legitimation Crisis*, p. 75.

21. Habermas, *Legitimation Crisis*, p. 76.

22. Habermas, *Legitimation Crisis*, pp. 85–86. For an interesting discussion of the politics of modernist art, see Thomas Dumm, "The Politics of Post-Modern Aesthetics: Habermas contra Foucault" (*Political Theory*, forthcoming).

23. Habermas, *Legitimation Crisis*, p. 70.

24. Habermas, *Legitimation Crisis*, p. 70.

25. The claim is, of course, that without humanly devised pharmaceuticals the medical and consumption goods of modern life would be impossible.

26. Habermas, *Legitimation Crisis*, p. 78.

27. Habermas, *Legitimation Crisis*, p. 108.

28. Habermas, *Legitimation Crisis*, p. 110.

29. Jürgen Habermas, *Knowledge and Human Interests* (Boston: Beacon, 1971), p. 307.

30. Henning Ottman, "Cognitive Interests and Self-Reflection," in *Habermas: Critical Debates*, ed. John Thompson and David Held (Cambridge: MIT Press, 1982), p. 81.

31. Because all action presupposes a historical context, we have a practical interest "in the preservation and expansion of the intersubjectivity of possible action-orienting mutual understanding" (Habermas, *Knowledge and Human Interests*, p. 310). Because human action implies interaction or coming to terms with other actors, we have an interest in attaining consensus, an interest in communication. This interest is rooted in an imperative of sociocultural life: "The survival of societal individuals is linked to the existence of a reliable intersubjectivity of understanding in ordinary language communication" (Thomas McCarthy, *The Critical Theory of Jürgen Habermas* [Cambridge: MIT Press, 1978], pp. 68–69).

Although Habermas rejects *Geist*, he adopts the Hegelian point that the knowing subject must be comprehended in its historical development. The modern subject is the outcome of the self-formative processes of both the species and the individual. Through the historical development of an ever-deepening self-consciousness, the modern subject is the author of himself and his deeds in a way that the self of Robust Faith could never be.

32. The emancipatory interest is less intuitively available than the technical or practical interests. It is based upon Habermas's theory of communication, which attempts to show that subjects already have, through language use, an idea of rational or nondistorted communication. We rely on this implicit understanding when we make a distinction, upon reflection, between oppressive and rational social institutions. Our ability to make this distinction expresses our interest in rational emancipation from

oppressive social structures. Another expression of the emancipatory power of self-reflection is in psychoanalysis, where a patient, through talking therapy, is freed from internal repression. Because we have the capacity for self-reflection and language, we have an interest in autonomy and responsibility that can free us from ideological and psychological illusions. This emancipatory interest, however, can find its ultimate realization only in a social setting itself free from institutions of domination.

33. Jürgen Habermas, *Toward a Rational Society* (Boston: Beacon, 1970), p. 83.

34. Habermas, *Rational Society*, p. 87.

35. McCarthy, p. 111.

36. McCarthy, p. 118.

37. Habermas, *Knowledge and Human Interests*, p. 130.

38. Jürgen Habermas, "A Reply to My Critics," in *Habermas: Critical Debates*, p. 241.

39. Habermas, "Reply," p. 244.

40. Habermas, "Reply," p. 248.

41. Habermas, "Reply," p. 248.

42. Habermas, "Reply," p. 248.

43. A full discussion of Habermas's argument for these claims must refer back to the whole of his theory of legitimation; I mention next only one of his more important conclusions.

44. Steven Lukes, "Of Gods and Demons: Habermas and Practical Reason," in *Habermas: Critical Debates*, pp. 137–38.

45. William E. Connolly, "The Dilemma of Legitimacy," in *Legitimacy and the State*, pp. 237–38.

46. Habermas, again when pressed, likewise speaks of an irreducible moment of otherness in nature, but his theory of the state assumes a technologically dominated nature. Lowi shares Habermas's views of reason and nature without the benefit of philosophical second thoughts.

47. Rüdiger Bubner elaborates this point in "Habermas's Concept of Critical Theory," in *Habermas: Critical Debates*, p. 52:

> Even if one concedes that an ideal does not always correspond to reality, the ideal must nevertheless be meaningful as an ideal. That is, it must be an appropriate criterion for testing whether a reality is inadequate, insofar as the reality must correspond to the ideal, at least in principle.

48. Habermas, "Reply," p. 236.

49. Habermas, "Reply," p. 235.

50. Habermas, *Legitimation Crisis*, p. 89.

51. Habermas, *Legitimation Crisis*, p. 37.

52. Charles Taylor, *Hegel* (Cambridge: Cambridge University Press, 1975), p. 544.

53. Taylor, *Hegel*, p. 546.

54. Charles Taylor, "The Politics of the Steady State," in *Beyond Indus-*

trial Growth, ed. Abraham Rotstein (Toronto: University of Toronto Press, 1976), p. 53.

55. Taylor, "Steady State," p. 66.
56. Charles Taylor, "Socialism and Weltanschauung," in *The Socialist Idea*, ed. Leszek Kolakowski and Stuart Hampshire (New York: Basic, 1974), p. 56.
57. Taylor, "Steady State," p. 60.
58. Taylor, "Steady State," p. 53.
59. Taylor, "Steady State," p. 63.
60. Taylor, "Steady State," p. 63.
61. Taylor, "Steady State," p. 64.
62. Taylor, "Steady State," p. 63.
63. Taylor, *Hegel*, p. 552.
64. Taylor, *Hegel*, p. 552.
65. Taylor, *Hegel*, p. 556.
66. See Taylor, *Hegel*, p. 558:

Marx's variant of "absolute" freedom is at the base of Bolshevik voluntarism which . . . has crushed all obstacles in its path with extraordinary ruthlessness, and has spawned again that terror which Hegel described with uncanny insight.

67. Taylor, *Hegel*, p. 561.
68. Taylor, *Hegel*, p. 540.
69. Charles Taylor, "What Is Human Agency?" in *The Self*, ed. Theodore Mischel (Oxford: Basil Blackwell, 1977), pp. 124–25.
70. Charles Taylor, "Language and Human Nature," A. P. Plaunt Memorial Lecture, Carleton University, 1978, p. 16.
71. Taylor, "Language," p. 22.
72. Taylor, "Human Agency," p. 126.
73. Charles Taylor, "Connolly, Foucault and Truth," *Political Theory* 13 (August 1985), p. 7.
74. Charles Taylor, "Understanding in Human Science," *Review of Metaphysics* 34 (September 1980), p. 32.
75. Taylor, "Human Science," p. 53.
76. Taylor, "Human Science," p. 48.
77. Taylor, "Human Science," p. 36.
78. Taylor, *Hegel*, p. 569.
79. Taylor, *Hegel*, p. 564.
80. Taylor, *Hegel*, p. 563.
81. Taylor, *Hegel*, p. 563.
82. Taylor, *Hegel*, p. 564.
83. Taylor, *Hegel*, p. 571.
84. Taylor, "Human Science," p. 34.
85. Taylor, "Human Science," p. 34.
86. See Taylor's *Philosophical Papers: Human Agency and Language*,

vol. 1 (Cambridge: Cambridge University Press, 1985), and *Philosophical Papers: Philosophy and the Human Sciences*, vol. 2 (Cambridge: Cambridge University Press, 1985), for essays on these topics and the structure of argument they share.

CHAPTER 4

UNTHINKING
FAITH AND ENLIGHTENMENT

Mutual Adversaries

A T the root of this study is the assumption that Hegel's dialectic of Faith and Enlightenment is a profound account of two historical modes of consciousness and the play between them. I have pursued the possibility that the terms of this dialectic continue to set a frame for contemporary political discourse and have found that the interpretation of environmentalism and state theory as heirs to the Faith-Enlightenment struggle yields unusual kernels of insight.[1]

The orientation to nature assumed by a theory significantly shapes that theory: to conceive nature as raw material for use and mastery is to be able to advocate environmental management, juridical democracy, and the rational state; to conceive nature as ordered in fundamental harmony with human needs makes possible the ideals of natural holism and the attuned state. A conception of nature does not, of course, determine the conceptions of self, knowledge, politics, and freedom within a perspective. It helps to enable them, however, and it is the one least thematized in contemporary political theory and therefore most illuminating to uncover.

We have also seen that each of the dominant voices in these debates is flawed and that blind spots are a function of the dynamic between disputants—each set of flaws is constituted in conjunction with its other. Deficiencies in natural holism prompt replies by environmental management that strengthen the initial position of management; inadequacies of masterful theories of the state are noted, remedied, and incorporated into an attuned theory. But blind spots remain: neither can redress its own flaws without compromising its insights. Put more broadly, each position crystallizes in response to its opponent as each dramatizes elements of a theory needed but unavailable to the other.

To see this is to recognize an internal connection between mutually acclaimed adversaries. Each is other-determined, asserting a set of insights designed to expose inadequacies in the other. The disputants are partners as well in an unwitting conspiracy to maintain the established terms of debate, for the holist-Promethean grooves of contemporary thought discourage thinking outside of them. There is another affinity between the opponents yet to be discussed, the orientation to "otherness."

Faith, Enlightenment, and Otherness

My treatment of each debate began with a critique of a Promethean perspective and concluded with a critique of the harmonious ontology of most anti-Promethean critiques. I will now review these two sets of critiques to develop their implications.

Natural holism argued that even the most sophisticated version of environmental management is unable to reverse environmental deterioration because it retains a view of nature as standing reserve. A management framework cannot generate respect for nature, a respect for its mysteries and unintelligibilities. When it does begin to recognize the difficulties with a conception of nature as standing reserve, it typically elaborates an ethic of rights for the environment. Yet this ethic affords respect to animal life only to the degree that it approaches the standard of human subjectivity; it still conceives nature in anthropocentric terms. In short, environmental management pursues the audacious project of reorganizing nature, denaturing beings and processes amenable to domestication and humanization, and extinguishing those that are not. It fails as an ethic of being in the world, claims the holist, in that it cannot respect elements in nature not easily explained or transformed by technique.

Expressivism offered a similar critique of a Promethean orientation to the state: its belief that a state with the power to rationalize society can also be a state that leaves its citizens free is naive; its obsession with instrumental rationality reduces holist protest to nostalgia or romanticism; its tendency to identify repression with less self-conscious forms of authority blinds it to the underside of its own project of rational mastery. Masterful theories of the state do not explore the suspicion that the increasing rationalization of social life alienates, divorcing us from the spiritual, imaginative, and other nonrational aspects of ourselves and our world. Thus, a Promethean state will be a repressive state: untoward elements of the self, the social order, and nature will be smothered in a sticky web of external (technocratic) or internal (socialized) control. Masterful theories, claims the expressivist, aim to install respect for persons, but their passion for coordination results in disrespect for modes of self-expression that do not or may not live up to a narrowed standard of rationality.

The holist critique of both forms of Prometheanism can now be stated more cogently: the demand for a world according to human reason does violence to that in nature and in the self resistant to rational order.

But the affirmative side of holism does not hold up as well as its critique. This study has been critical of the holist alternative, for although holism claims that with philosophical subtlety and existential humility the nonrational need not be mastered but can be accommodated, much more than subtlety and humility is required to sustain holist positions—the assumption of an ontological harmony is also needed.

The holist charge in chapter 2 was that environmental management was anthropocentric, unable to respect or even conceive nature on its own terms. But I argued that holistic respect was linked to the view that nature is designed for us and we designed to fit it. Natural holism can bear the burden of accommodating nature only on the condition that it be a garden planted for humans. Does not this Ptolemaic insistence, that humans be at the center of the universe, also exhibit a certain anthropocentrism?

And in chapter 3 Taylor offered a powerful critique of both the individualist and the collectivist ideals as polities with no room to breathe, as orders that demand too much organization and precision out of beings and social processes not fully susceptible to administrative rationality. But Taylor's alternative ideal presupposes the view that attunement to a natural bent of things is possible and that self-fulfillment and freedom depend upon such attunement. The presumptuous demand within the theory of attunement is that humans inhabit a world predisposed to them. Would the attuned state offer more breathing space to benign disorder or nonrational eccentricities, or would it target them as instances of selves and social processes in special need of reconciliation with the natural, beneficent bent?

Chapters 2 and 3 suggested an eerie affinity between the holist and Promethean projects; I can now state this affinity explicitly. Neither can tolerate otherness—that in nature and the self which does not bear the mark of human or divine rationality. Each depreciates elements of life not readily susceptible to mastery or harmonization. It is clear how this intolerance operates within a Promethean theory, but my claim is that neither does a harmonious holism aspire to let otherness be.

The concept of otherness is inimical to a harmonious holism. If the world is a rational design or a naturally harmonious unity, there is no such thing as otherness—that which does not fit or which makes no sense—there is only that which appears not to fit or to mean, and this stain will fade as faith in the larger order intensifies. While aspects of being may appear to mortals as alien, they are in truth integral parts of a world to which we can become attuned, for otherness cannot be an ontological condition.

And this points to a way in which a harmonious holism, while correct in its exposé of Promethean hubris, is itself not nearly humble enough—or is capable of humility only on the assumption of a beautifully designed world. Natural holists and theorists of attunement seek to identify otherness but not to let it be. While asserting to the Promethean that the domination of the unordered remainder of life (the nonrational) can only drive it underground, they themselves propose a method for reducing it.

If the Promethean longs to master otherness, the holist yearns to bring it into attunement with an enriched self and a more responsive social world. A Promethean seeks to impose human form upon otherness, denying or suppressing it; a holist seeks to bind its identity to a larger unity, assimilating it and defining resistance to assimilation as inauthenticity or an expression of subjectivism. The insistent demand (the naive faith) of one is that the world will succumb to human control; the insistent demand (the naive faith) of the other is that otherness will reveal some link to an authentic whole.

The perspective from which this critique springs is the heir of neither Faith nor Enlightenment: otherness could not exist in a designed world, and it is a warrant for mastery in an enlightened one. Nor does it spring from the Hegelian solution to the Faith-Enlightenment impasse, the ontology of *Geist*. It is a perspective that, if it had to be assigned one source, is Nietzschean. I propose now a theoretical exercise to deepen my account of this perspective—a look at the Faith-Enlightenment dialectic through the eyes of Michel Foucault, a theorist quite at home with the vocabulary of otherness. I will then return to the question of ethics, a question that Foucault only begins to develop: Can there be an orientation to self and nature that is not destructive of the nonrational and nonrationalizable elements therein and that does not, implicitly or explicitly, assume the world to be user-friendly?

The Dialectic According to Foucault

While a robust faith could indeed enchant the world for a while, it could not be sustained. Robust Faith was, from a Foucauldian perspective, a fanciful superimposition upon a world not itself designed to fulfill human fantasies:

We must not imagine that the world turns toward us a legible face which we would have only to decipher; the world is not the accomplice of our knowledge; there is no prediscursive providence which disposes the world in our favor.[2]

The flaws in Faith identified by Enlightenment—for example, a confusion of the material and the immaterial through a system of resemblances, an adoration of historically contingent forms—were not seen by Enlightenment for what they were: evidence of the world's recalcitrance to human knowledge and control. They were seen merely as evidence of an excessively naive attempt to read a world legible only through careful scientific observation. Enlightenment itself was not ready to draw the more radical conclusion that world and self are multiplicities that would resist secular as well as religious unification. Despite this retention of a creationist ontology, the Enlightenment turned a corner: by challenging the decaying faith, it opened the way for those like Foucault to assert the thesis of radical disharmony and explore its implications.

The new, post-Enlightenment self was a more self-assertive being, says Foucault, for he replaced the debunked confidence in God with an equally comforting confidence in self. But self-assertion later lost its soothing quality as individuals came to the chilling conclusion that self-assertion was all that stood between them and a nature indifferent to human needs, opaque to the quest for complete knowledge, and resistant to control.

The modern self, then, assumed an attitude of nervous engagement with the present, a self-assigned task of world inquisition, of thematization. Always alert now for signs of that which lay below the threshold of awareness (and is thus potentially dangerous), moderns relentlessly forge "topics," "fields of study," "subject matters." Modes of relating to self, others, and nature are transformed from underground wanderings to categories and theories, for only so enclosed can unreliable elements be brought into the open and under control. The relation between background cultural understandings and idiosyncratic thoughts is thematized as the struggle between "tradition" and "liberty"; group labor using available instrumentalities turns into "relations of production" lodged inside a "mode of production"; notions of death or God are now tested for the efficacy of "myth" or the coherence of "theology." Thematization permeates modern life: "For the first time in history . . . the fact of living was no longer an inaccessible substrate that only emerged from time to time, amid the randomness of death and its fatality."[3] The biological bases of human existence—human bodies, their collaboration as pairs and as a species—can form a "sexuality" and a "population."

Of course, preEnlightenment selves also placed life within some frame, but the intensity (perhaps desperation) of the modern attitude and the extent of its thematic reach into life set it apart. The Enlightenment debunking of Faith's tradition, the application of what Hegel called negative critique to religion, superstition, and custom, was at the same time a crystallization of "religion," "superstition," and "custom"—for these notions are themselves products of a drive for thematic self-consciousness, from this Foucauldian perspective. In contrast to Platonic or Christian systematic thought, modern thought employs a veritable methodology of thematization—no longer is it necessary to deploy critique in the service of some ideal, for digging up ground becomes liberating in itself. To open up new possibilities is to achieve the freedom available to us.

But for Foucault, this modern project of thematization cuts two ways. First, the surgical cut:

To thematize is to clarify or give specificity to a process or entity, to make an intelligible form out of a liquid one. Organizing a diffuse or loosely conglomerated mass into a system bestows identity, producing as an individuated unity that which was inchoate or perhaps stable but unrecognizably so. In short, modern thematization is a self-conscious art that creates a meaningful, comfortable, and comforting world. And that is no mean achievement.

To thematize is also to extend the realm of public action, admirably enhancing the possibility of social change. Gender, race, the economy, the environment—phenomena formerly the province of fate or the reflection of nongeneralizable interests—have been organized into political issues, their established forms constituted as mere conventions. Both the cause and the effect of this politicization is an increasing awareness that the categories and beliefs we employ, the roles we play, even the natural objects against which we define our selves, are significantly human-made. And if human finitude and fallibility are insinuated into the very fabric of the world, then it can be rewoven. It is possible, then, to construct more equitable, more just, or less dangerous social forms.

Now the wound. Let us recall the expressivist's protest against thematization before we explore the Foucauldian warning, for the latter is a critical response to expressivism.

The relentless thematization characteristic of the modern age is nothing but the quest for rational mastery of the world! cries the theorist of attunement. This quest takes on a new urgency with the historical demise of Faith, for Enlightenment attempted to use reason to reintegrate the world as a meaningful whole. Although reintegration is itself an admirable goal, the heirs of Enlightenment are mistaken if they believe reason sufficient to fill God's shoes. Moreover, because life is more than reason, life can become rational only at the expense of richness, color, and beauty. Modern thematizers have created a world wherein thinking (that indefinable ability to judge, sense, ponder, wonder, explore) has been reduced to the calculation of efficient means. Thought qua instrumental rationality has become the privileged banner flown in every district of life. Techno-utilitarianism flourishes in politics, architecture, economics, occupational life, while spirituality, aesthetics, or noncognitive experience is denigrated, ignored, or repressed.

The world of Robust Faith, continues the expressivist, was not tyrannized by instrumental rationality, for it incorporated the nonrational into a cosmology. True, this cosmology is not available to us in its robust form, for the belief in a world of signs is incompatible with our acknowledgment of the extent of human participation in self and world. But Faith is not dead! cries the expressivist as he seeks to reconstitute Faith as both modern and nonrationalist, both tenable and efficacious as a cosmology. The expressivist revises the strong teleology of Robust Faith in several ways.

First, although the existence of telos in self and nature cannot be guaranteed, the expressivist avers that it remains a possibility. One cannot definitively refute the possibility that there is a direction in being that is both discernible to some extent and capable of some degree of guidance. This possibility "doesn't seem . . . to be in worse shape than its obvious rivals."[4] Second, the theorist of attunement shifts the locus of telos from an enchanted nature to a self with an inherent bent. For can we not apprehend a difference between more and less authentic interpretations of self? Third, although this telos may be even more difficult to divine (since nature is no longer filled with divine signs), the expressivist seeks a clearer and more self-conscious articulation of it. That is, because moderns will not be convinced of an ontological bent if it is presented as an inexplicable mystery, expressivism must show how a weak telos in the self is compatible with some version of science and reason.

We are now in a position to compare the Foucauldian critique of thematization to the expressivist one. For Foucault there is indeed a dark side to the thematizing project, but it is not the problem of excessive faith in instrumental rationality. The subjugation of that which resists a rationalist definition is only one instance of the subjugation that accompanies any imposition of order. It is misleading to reduce the problem to instrumental rationality, for each and every form of categorical organization, however expressive or antiinstrumental, will be exclusionary in some way. Thematization enlightens and politicizes, extending the realm of conscious human management; at the same time, thematization enlightens and subjugates, torturing the space for the nonmanageable. Promethean and holist modes of thematization both cut two ways, and *neither* is sensitive enough to the wounds it creates.

Thematization is a necessary imposition of form, doing violence to selves and natural systems which resist the mold! cries the Foucauldian. The world of Robust Faith was not innocent of this violence, but neither was it as efficient in producing or applying it. Because the fundamental organization of life had already been accomplished through divine intentions, only a loose or thin thread of human thematization was called for. And if enchanted life, compared to modern life, was brought into the sphere of human administration only superficially and sporadically—if power had not achieved its present "economy"—then that which appeared anomalous would be less efficiently managed. Foucault's discussions of earlier methods for defining and responding to the lawbreaker and the madman illustrate this point.[5]

And the effects of the Enlightenment canonization of reason are more pernicious than the expressivist knows, continues Foucault. It is not simply that passion or imagination is devalued (in a sense both are elevated, if compartmentalized, as an important accompaniment to the rational self). The most important effect of the precise and pervasive thematization of the modern age is the accelerated production of otherness, those forms of nonrationality or resistance less positively valued than passion or imagination. This thematization insists that difference expose itself to punishment or reformation. Unreason is the victim, but it is not a victim of benign neglect or even denigration, as the expressivist implies. Unreason is reconstituted as the irrational in need of rigorous prevention, detection, inspection, intervention, therapy, treatment, cure, defeat.

In their clamor to locate difference within the categories of rationality and normality, rationalist thematizers do not explore the suspicion that the increasing rationalization of social life helps to foster more forms of deviance in need of regulation. In their quest to extend the sphere of legality into new areas of life, they help to foster new illegalities in need of apprehension and punishment. Thematization turns difference into deviance, and that is its truly black effect.

The Enlightenment expansion of thematization was not the wrong means to the benign end of reintegrating otherness, as the expressivist believes. It was the targeting and subjugation of a resistance that would refuse to go away even were spirituality and aesthetics to be valorized, even if the revised, more modestly teleological cosmology were installed. The expressivist critique is correct to oppose Enlightenment rationalism, but it fails to develop an understanding of the link between rationalization and normalization. This link exists because life and world are always partially other to us and because otherness is not fully susceptible to containment or assimilation.

Foucault's account of the modern deployment of "sexuality" exemplifies this counterthesis. Sexuality, he argues, is a thematic construction that codifies the body and forces a unity upon its multiple pleasures. Sexuality disciplines and normalizes a desiring body that Foucault conceives as a cacophony of "organs, somatic localizations, functions, anatomo-physiological systems, sensations, and pleasures."[6] The history of our treatment (both exploitive and therapeutic) of bodies that fall outside the norm—gays, hermaphrodites, nymphomaniacs, neuters, dwarfs, giants—is a history of the violence required by the institutionalization of sexuality.

The thematic of sexuality rationalizes and normalizes the self— but leaves sickness and deviance in its wake. And the subjugation involved in sexualization is not confined to those bodies or desires that do not fit the norm. Even those that apparently do are interned, for to be a modern self with a sexuality is to be condemned to a wild-goose chase in pursuit of a true nature, an authentic self that lies, we are told, beneath our repressed sexuality. Sexuality is a lie, a construction that pretends to be natural in order to do its dirty work (normalization) more effectively. Through an intricate system of psychiatric, therapeutic, medical, commercial, and religious institutions, we are lured to the belief that our sexuality is a political prisoner and that an authentic existence depends upon liberating it from the confines of Puritan morality, Victorian prudishness, or bourgeois superficiality.

For Foucault, however, there is no true self to be found, if truth is the discovery of some self-essence that finally enables a harmonious identity. There is no unified self beneath. Through the deployment of sexuality,

we have arrived at the point where we expect our intelligibility to come from what was for many centuries thought of as madness; the plentitude of our body from what was long considered its stigma . . . ; our identity from what was perceived as an obscure and nameless urge.[7]

Sexuality is a fictitious reality with imposing effects. Because no natural harmony exists, any imposed harmony must be enforced by strategies like the Lowian, the Habermasian, the Tayloresque—by proliferating laws and regulations or by insidiously internalized norms. The latter are especially pernicious, for in modernity norms, like instrumental rationality, constantly seek to expand their terrain.

Foucault shares the expressivist's admiration for the way the world of Robust Faith could accept a greater share of the inexplicable, and he also agrees that Robust Faith entails too little self-consciousness to be tenable today. But the theory of attunement misconstrues the enchanted solution to otherness: expressivism claims that otherness was integrated and thereby dissolved into a harmonious ontology, that in the world of Robust Faith there was no otherness to violate. But otherness or recalcitrant material, claims Foucault, was not absent from the enchanted world—it was simply less thematized. Thematization increases the need to "do something" about otherness, though it does not cause otherness; Robust Faith allowed otherness to roam a little, but it could not (and neither can we) dissolve it in a higher unity or transform it into an inherently meaningful substance.

Expressivism's misinterpretation of Robust Faith, its nostalgia for a world lost, gives it hope that a semblance of attunement can be recaptured. But Foucault repudiates this hope. Despite expressivism's modification of the teleological stance, it still clings to what is most in need of abandonment: the notion that self and nature are unified and truth-revealing. Expressivism still conceives life too much in terms of

man's concrete essence, the realization of his potential. . . . The "right" to life, to one's body, to health, to happiness, to the satisfaction of needs . . . beyond all the oppressions or "alienation," the "right" to rediscover what one is and all that one can be.[8]

To have a robust faith in God or nature is to rest easy that the cosmos is in order, and this makes the Promethean project less compelling. The stronger the teleological claim, the weaker the Promethean urge. Both Taylor and Foucault agree on this. They also agree that strong teleological claims are unacceptable to self-conscious, modern agents. But even weak teleological claims are unacceptable to Foucault, who sees them as comforting self-delusions, as a form of homesickness.

A world of Robust Faith would not require a social order as highly organized as our own and hence would allow for more spaces beyond the purview of rational control. Taylor would agree with Foucault on this. The bearers of unreason, mystery, or eccentricity could inhabit these unthematized spaces in relative peace. But this could only be an unintended consequence, for the faithful would not thematize otherness as a concern since for them concord with being lies within the soul of difference. And thus Taylor would probably take issue with Foucault's description of the virtues of a world of faith.

Foucault provokes the question, "How can we relate ethically to otherness once we eschew teleological pretensions and discern the ambiguous character of modern thematization?" Both Foucault and Taylor empower my response.[9]

Fractious Holism

The aim is to articulate an ethic of greater tolerance for otherness in nature and in the social order. But an ethic connects with a more fundamental view of the possibilities open for ethical action, that is, with a set of ontological assumptions. I call the set postulated here "fractious holism."

"Holism" because both human and nonhuman elements of the world, both intelligent and intelligible dimensions of life, are interconnected, constituted in part by their relations to one another. They form a whole where a shift in any one element has effects on every other. This study has been alert to the ways in which humans are engendered and constrained by linguistic, institutional, bodily, and natural-environmental contexts and the ways in which these contexts are formed in part by the character of human participation in them. Moreover, these contexts have a certain stability. Kohak, Compton, and Taylor are right to insist on these points. "Holism" also because we can speak, very generally, of persistent circumstances of human existence—the longing to be at home in the world, the sociality and technique it spawns, the bodily-perceptual field that is the condition of possibility of time, space, subject, and object.

The holism is "fractious" because the complex whole is not entirely coherent or harmonious. The ontological view I play out here is of a world far from chaotic, but perhaps even further from a state of harmonious integration. Thus, a modifier that speaks to the existence of otherness, of recalcitrance within the world, is needed.

The runner-up is "entropic," as it is used in thermodynamics to mean "descriptive of the amount of energy in a system not available for doing work." Energy not available for work is, I think, an apt description of that which escapes our categories, refuses to be disciplined to our satisfaction, and walks out on its assigned job of providing meaning. But I fear that the term "entropy" suggests also a tendency toward uniformity, toward homogenized disarray. This connotation is inappropriate, for it insinuates a world both too disordered and too docile; it lacks a sense of the defiance, dissonance, or indomitability of elements within the whole.

Thus, the ontology I postulate is a fractious holism, for it always includes elements that "tend to cause trouble by opposition to an established order," "interfere with its smooth operation," "are likely to function in unpredictable ways." To be fractious is to be disposed to make breaches, to interrupt good feeling or harmony. An ethic of otherness would have to abide by this ontology, in a sense be expressive of it.

What might it mean to live a life particularly alert to that which persistently resists our insistent imposition of form upon it? How does one relate ethically to a fractious but interdependent world?

Awe

Awe might play a central role. Respect for otherness could issue from the awe inspired by that which is strange, bizarre, powerfully nonrational. A fractious holist ethic would endorse contact with otherness in the self—with "freaks," "deviants," "geniuses," "the insane," and with that in every individual which is resistant to rational interpretation or control, opaque to social normalization—in the hope that contact would inspire awe.

The fractious holist would also advocate expanded opportunities for contact with wilderness, for in the wilderness one could be awed at the sight of gigantic mountains or the feel of a mighty waterfall or total, silent darkness. Here fractious holism coincides with Kohak's world of harmonies. The awesome experience of nature makes explicit one dimension of otherness: that which is other possesses characteristics, powers, or potentialities simply unavailable to humans. We cannot fly like a condor or shine like the sun; we cannot flow like a waterfall or erupt like a volcano—except, of course, metaphorically. And the prevalence of these types of metaphors is evidence of the extent to which nature provides the background of human identity; we define ourselves by contrast and comparison to it, and we enrich our imagination through metaphors derived from it. Its otherness is crucial to our identity. To see nature as standing reserve is to deny this important connection between self-identity, creativity, and nature-as-difference. To treat it merely as standing reserve is to lose the fund of difference from which rich identities are forged and sustained.

Environmental management also rejects the view that humans and the world upon which they act are both of the same design, but it concludes that the world is intrinsically valueless matter, valuable only insofar as it can be rendered useful. A fractious holist ethic, an ethic of awe, presents a secular alternative to this utilitarianism. It can regard elements in nature and self alien to rationality as valuable reminders of the limits of human reason. It can appreciate the natural and bodily world as an ambiguous setting in which we reside, as both a medium and an impediment to human fulfillment, as successively host and adversary.

An ethic based on awe contains no guarantees, however. Although awe is a potent experience, it is by nature an infrequent one. And it may not be potent enough to overcome the desire to make a home in the world by mastering it. Neither does awe always inspire tolerance, for the object of awe can easily turn into an awful object—things strange can repel and disgust as well as fascinate and attract. In other words, the link between the experience of estrangement and respect for the strange, between awe and tolerance, is tenuous. And it is not clear that an ethics of awe would triumph over an orientation of disgust and mastery once the insistence on assimilating unharmonious elements was relaxed.

There is another difficulty with an ethic based upon awe. The experience of awe tends to exaggerate the autonomy of otherness, for it presents the other as an independent object to be contemplated from afar. But otherness, as it is conceived from within a fractious holist ontology, is at once something that hits us in the face from "out there" and something we are always in the process of making. A stream becomes "other" when it interferes with a standard plan for a housing project; an aesthetically insignificant stand of trees becomes "other" when it threatens to grow into power lines; an uninspiring child with a short attention span becomes a hyperactive "other" when childhood is organized around school and school organized around a nine-to-three schedule; a woman whose body is strong and hairy becomes a sexual "other" when we thematize femininity as thin and smooth.

To reiterate the Foucauldian point made earlier: with each attempt to instill discipline, regularity, unity, and predictability into our lives, with each advance in thematization and control, we generate that which does not fit. But we cannot help but generate otherness, for the world was not designed with humans at the top of a biotic pyramid. In short, it is natural for humans to alter the course of nature, and these alterations do some violence.

To thematize thematization is to see it as both necessary and destructive: we sculpt a niche for ourselves in a world partly at odds with our projects, and in so doing we generate otherness in the self and the world that resists our designs. This reflexive realization contains an acknowledgment of our share of responsibility for otherness. Perhaps this sense of responsibility can inspire greater tolerance.

For example, if I recognize that my identity is the product of a self-imposed regimentation of a diverse and conflicting set of desires, drives, impulses, thoughts, and intentions, if I take myself "as the object of a complex and difficult elaboration,"[10] I may be easier on my self when the conflict reignites and my elaboration begins to unravel. To be sure, the modern ideal of self-control urges one "not to accept oneself as one is in the flux of the passing moments,"[11] but if the self is understood as an edifice constantly under materially imposed as well as artist-imposed renovation (and not the expression of a naturally solid unity), one can come to appreciate it for its refreshing changeability as well as for its comforting dimensions of stability. No longer able to base tolerance of otherness on innocence about otherness, we can perhaps obtain a measure of tolerance through self-conscious acknowledgment of our unavoidable role in engendering it.

One can extend this psychology to an orientation to politics. If the social order is understood as a precarious and subjugating achievement, perhaps an experimental attitude is best, for we cannot know in advance the concrete consequences for otherness of a policy agenda. Whether the aim is to tear down old institutions or devise new ones, the fractious world is expressed best through an engaged attitude that creates unities, judges the extent of the damage, and begins again. To treat the political order as a dangerous work of art is to ensure a restless, contentious, and lively form of politics.

Although this conception of politics has in some ways outgrown the holist-Promethean dynamic, it also grows out of it. It does not repudiate all prior political tacks, but it does seek distance from the claim of all to be cohesive, coherent orientations. The political stance of this new path might dismantle an old program or might endorse it as the best of the bad alternatives; it might advocate policies formerly considered illegitimate; and it might even introduce some not considered at all.

Politics and Freedom

A political stance in a world of fractious holism must be experimental and tentative if it is to acknowledge that any political stance enables as well as subjugates. Thus, the fractious holist is reluctant to elaborate abstract principles except the principle of local, experimental, and tentative action. This is, of course, exceedingly difficult to do, especially for the political theorist of fractious holism. I will now ignore this warning to speak only about concrete particulars and hazard a statement on the fractious-holist conception of freedom.

Freedom involves breaking up reified unities like "the responsible agent" or "the sexual person" and transgressing historically imposed limits to what we can be. To be concerned with freedom is to uncover the particular, the contingent, and the finite in limits defined by the order as universal or necessary. It is to deploy a genealogical critique.

But to show a limit to be contingent is not necessarily to repudiate it. A fractious-holist conception of freedom does not deny the necessity of limits, nor does it portray limits as mere errors; to do so would render it vulnerable to Hegel's critique of absolute freedom. The fractious-holist conception of freedom, like the ideal of a general will, does seek to expose social institutions as constructions and to remold them, but it sees reform as incapable of reconciling self and order and as always involved in the production of new otherness in need of remedy—for any newly imposed social structure will also have effects threatening to or exclusive of some aspects of some of the entities touched by it.

Freedom for a fractious holist also requires taking responsibility for the edifices one is only in part responsible for creating. One is only in part responsible because some terms of our actions have been set by history and others by the recalcitrant material worked upon—bodies, nature. Freedom is not the denial of limits but the problematization of the particular readings we give to them. The appropriate ethical orientation to this recalcitrant material, then, is to place it within some frame while trying to keep that frame loose enough to tolerate protest from that which does not fit. The ambiguous commitment to ends and agendas and to that which strains against them provides the context of freedom.

It is clear how an ethic expressive of fractious holism can, through genealogy, seek out and expose contingencies and arbitrary constraints; it is less clear what I mean by the term "recalcitrant material." What can be said about the status of the material the human thematizer has to work with? What can be known about the form or structure of the world that humans seek to act upon, harmonize with, control, or use?

It is difficult for the ethic I seek to speak in general terms about the contours of the "material" of self and world. Its holism demands that it say something in order to distinguish itself from radical subjectivism or the empiricism of discrete facts; its understanding of the inevitability of otherness demands that it not say so much that it lapses back into harmonious holism. Perhaps we can take a cue on this issue from Foucault:

there is always something in the social body, in classes, groups and individuals themselves which in some sense escapes . . . something which is by no means a more or less docile or reactive primal matter, but rather a centrifugal movement, an inverse energy, a discharge.[12]

In opposition to harmonious holism's view of the material as "being," as having a definite, discernible, and intelligible bent, Foucault can say that it has a diffuse resistance discernible only negatively. That is to say, the limits to molding this material, while having a certain definitiveness, are usually recognizable only after they have been violated—after it is too late for attunement. I will say (although Foucault might not) that the material has a resiliency even within its bent. When speaking abstractly, resistance is a force, an unnamed blockage to will; this blockage receives a name only when we move from a philosophical discourse to a political one—then it becomes "gays," "feminists," "mental patients," "rednecks," "fate," "accidents," and "contingencies."

Environmentalism

From within an ontology of fractious holism, any ethic that seeks reverence for the material of life, then, is inappropriate, for it asks too much of us to revere stuff whose accessibility is only diffuse resistance. Human subjects are capable of regard, even respect, for nonrationality and nonhumanity, but this capacity must dwindle the more the object of that regard is understood as alien, other.

Human life requires order, and there can be no human order without imposing form on humans and nature. Natural holism does not fully acknowledge this dilemma. An environmental ethic will fail if it demands, as the natural holist often does, that we love or revere nature—for our war against physical want and psychological uncertainty precludes the passivity of an orientation to nature that listens for sounds of natural harmony. Habermas is right to insist upon the technical interest, even if his version of it resides within a rationalistic philosophy of nature. Because nature is not designed to mesh perfectly with our needs, no matter how carefully and closely we listen to it, there is always a gap between the hospitality of nature and our demands as guests. This gap makes necessary at times an orientation to nature from the point of view of technical control.

To insist that the intrinsic value of nature be revered is to engender the opposite response—the further humanization of nature or the abandonment of the attempt to create an environmental ethic. To ask "How can we revere nature?" is to ask "How can we have order without otherness?" and to put the question in this way implies two equally unsatisfactory answers: Faith's dreamy response that we can assimilate otherness if only we believe in telos; Enlightenment's pragmatic response that life requires order, order generates otherness, thus mastery is justified.

The environmentalism of natural holism *is* unrealistic or untenable, as the environmental managers say, for it advocates the lifestyle of a gentleman farmer in a world of complex economic interdependencies that only a privileged few could hope to escape. The natural holist implies that the more primitive our technology, the more rudimentary our forms of social and economic organization, the more pastoral our lives, the better, for he believes that the most ethical orientation to nature is one that comes closest to some original, pure design. Because fractious holism rejects the equation of the order of nature with moral goodness, it does not need to reject all but the most primitive forms of technology.

But a fractious-holist environmentalism shares the natural-holist view that current forms of technology are too violent and too destructive of nature because our demands upon nature are too great. Like the steady-state and appropriate-technology[13] versions of natural holism, fractious holism endorses the attempt to reduce the demand that nature provide us with more and more material affluence. An environmental ethic must be coupled with public policies designed to move the economy away from planned obsolescence and limitless growth and toward a frugal, creative, recycling way of life. It must be connected as well to a redesign of institutions, work life, and architecture that allows us to experience in a positive way the otherness of nature.

For example, public buildings designed to open to the outside where possible, with natural lighting, would encourage us, every day and in a nonextraordinary way, to face the shelter and resistance that is nature. Windowless, temperature-controlled rooms cost more than the heating bills they were designed to reduce, and the price tag for the vast infrastructural support for private automobiles should include the social cost of discouraging another opportunity to experience the resistance of nature, namely, bicycling. The obsession with comfort, with protection from the elements, with cleanliness and deodorants, and with curing the slightest eccentricity or abnormality, has too often prevented experiences of otherness and of our contribution to it—experiences that could engender more appreciation of the limits to human science and technique and of the dangers that accompany the refusal to acknowledge these limits.

But the theory of the steady state must be detached from the harmonious longings of the communitarian, for the fractious holist is cognizant of the normalization required by the ideal of community. The fractious holist ought to reject community as a global aim and deploy it instead as a guide in specific political actions. We should muster up this thing called civic virtue when we can (civic virtue must play a part in the shift in the priorities of the political economy) but should acknowledge that we lose as well as gain by mobilizing this ideal.

A fractious-holist environmentalism asks: How can we curtail the insistent demand to order nature so thoroughly? How can we slow the demand for more and more masterful forms of technology? What is lost when we insist upon being the master of nature? It responds to these questions neither by reverting to an ontology of harmonious holism nor by insisting with harmonizers and managers alike that limits to our mastery of nature require such a dubious ontology. Respect for nature grows out of appreciation of the manifold points of difference between it and our designs, and an appreciation of ontologically grounded difference encourages us to set limits to the designs we would impose upon inner and outer nature.

But why should we set these limits? What justification can an ethic that seeks to express a fractious world give for its desire to tread lightly?

No justification with the force of a moral imperative is possible. We should tread lightly because it is the wisest orientation to a world upon which we depend but which we cannot fully comprehend or control. Even after the accelerated modern attempt, we have not mastered nature, so why not relieve ourselves of the dangerous and maddening Promethean obsession? Unless we do, we will continue to endure environmentally induced cancer; dwindling supplies of clean water, soil, and air; and the threat of nuclear winter. Human existence upon the planet is precarious, not guaranteed by nature or providence.

This fractious-holist claim that we are on our own to do the best we can will, I believe, strike a responsive chord in the mind of the contemporary political thinker. For it is this same claim that motivated the many versions of the "muddling through" thesis in political science literature. It speaks to the contemporary experience that patriotism, community, family, and love are not unqualified goods—that there is chauvinism in patriotism, authoritarianism in community, neurosis in family life, and jealousy and rage in love. We may be ripe for an ethic that explicitly acknowledges that allegiances to country, community, individuals (or schemes, themes, theories, beliefs) can never be absolute, never quite as fulfilling as anticipated. And to be a true fractious holist is to be doubly reflective about these ideals—it is to confess that we lose something by acknowledging the underside of our ideals: we lose the ease of our conscience and the freedom to act without tortured consideration of possible implications, long-term effects, dangerous unintended consequences.

Harmonious Holism and Fractious Holism

From a harmonious-holist perspective, the foregoing discussions of freedom and environmentalism simply don't wash. The attempt to give content to a limited but genealogical freedom and a reverenceless environmentalism are duplicitous: they require a conception of self and nature as multiple, as essenceless, and to conceive self and nature in this way—to be so reticent about inherent properties that pose limits to self-invention or nature-invention—is to disqualify a theory from the right to speak of *recalcitrant* material. And what is otherness if not recalcitrance, stubbornness, resistance, elusiveness?

According to the harmonious holist, a fractious holism underplays the solidity of personal identity. Evidence of this solidity is our ability to recognize gains in self-understanding, for this identification would be impossible were there nothing substantial to use as a standard of judgment. Thus, the very rejection of the possibility of harmonious integration is at odds with lived experience.

But the fractious-holist positions I have outlined affirm the claim that we can distinguish between better and worse self-interpretations. They do this, however, while denying that we must judge interpretations against the ideal of a fulfilled self. Rather, a self-interpretation should be judged good if it contributes to an appreciation of the artful character of our achievement; if it supports a work of art whose standards of beauty are not confined to "balance," "cohesion," "harmony," but include also "eccentricity," "things out of place." These latter elements form part of the ideal self of the fractious holist.

Neither can my fractious holism distinguish between better and worse social orders, continues the harmonious holist. If, for example, it endorses a less disciplined, less normalized society, it can only mean that such a society is truer in the sense of being expressive of, having a deeper affinity for, the essential characteristics of human being. And a fractious holist does not have access to this standard after a repudiation of telos in self and nature. But why could not one judge modern societies as better or worse according to the extent to which they offer space for otherness? A less normalized relation to the state, to the earth, or to one's body is better precisely because no relation can ever be deeply attuned, because the perfection of self and society are impossible and destructive dreams. Only perpetually incomplete self-creation is possible, a self-creation that is, no doubt, limited by internal resistance, external opposition, and an ethical concern for the otherness we help produce. So a society that admits this can challenge the hegemony of (but not destroy) the imperative to concretize the self and the political order. This is a better society, not a truer one.

In short, the debate between a harmonious holist and a fractious holist is a debate over the degree to which the world is unified and the degree to which we can recognize inherent limits to action and will. This text cannot settle this debate, for it cannot determine the truth of ontological assumptions. But it can explore the ethical-political implications of each. And saying this, I can agree with the harmonious holist that the radical antiharmony thesis exaggerates. Much of Foucault's work deploys such an exaggeration, thinking it necessary to play out "the possibility of no longer being, doing, or thinking what we are, do, think,"[14] that is, to lure us from the worn paths of Faith and Enlightenment.

But fractious holism diverges from the strongest version of Foucauldian theory. The orientation to otherness endorsed here is disharmonious in its espousal of the view that humans are incomplete beings in a world not created to complete their essence or fulfill their needs, and expressivist in its view that the affirmation of this disharmony can contribute to a more ethical politics, one more tolerant of difference.

A position that acknowledges only disharmony would magnify the disjunction between self and world and between self and self. Otherness within the self—that is, thoughts that take one by surprise, socially unacceptable urges, moods, rages, unexplained pains and depressions—would emerge on the same plane as those dispositions and principles that constitute the self as a subject. Likewise, the social order would appear as able to fulfill collective aims only by chance; nature would appear as a chaotic set of processes tenuously linked to the survival needs of humans. Such a picture would be so clear that it would distort; for the nonintentional and the prediscursive coexist within intentions and language; pains and moods are still bound up with the identities of the persons expressing them; the social order does touch and enhance (even if it does not complete or give ultimate meaning to) human existence; the earth is quite hospitable to perception and bodily functioning when compared to the natural environment of Mars or the sun. But these incomplete compatibilities ought not to be construed as evidence of design, or of the possibility of overcoming or assimilating otherness.

I find it necessary to modify the antiharmony thesis, for harmonious holism is right to call any talk of freedom nonsense from within a theory where the material of life is wholly unintelligible: Could we then be blamed for any harm done to it? How could we take responsibility for our imposing creations? Even Nietzsche is not committed to a radical antiharmony thesis.

One thing is needful. —To "give style" to one's character—a great and rare art! It is practiced by those who survey all the strengths and weaknesses of their nature and then fit them into an artistic plan. . . . Here a large mass of second nature has been added; there a piece of original nature has been removed—both times through long practice and daily work at it. Here the ugly that could not be removed is concealed; there it has been reinterpreted and made sublime. Much that is vague and resisted shaping has been saved and exploited for distant views; it is meant to beckon toward the far and immeasurable.[15]

Nietzsche's call to give style to one's character appreciates the way we both belong to and deface the world, and an ethic of fractious holism points in the same direction, believing that we must mess with the world, constrained by "original nature," but never conquer it. The beauty of this position is that it accepts that which is vague and resistant to shaping while giving it a place within the work of art—as a reminder that the self is not self-contained or self-sufficient, but exists alongside "the far and immeasurable."

Harmonious holism may be right that an ethic of fractious holism fails, that the desire to tolerate difference cannot be part of a view of the world as ultimately intractible, that there can be no expressivism that is not attuned to a world ready to be heard. But it is possible that we become more attuned to life and politics by giving up the wish to be at home in a world preattuned to us.

NOTES

1. Where might one go from here? One might dispute the efficacy of the

Faith-Enlightenment framework and develop alternative interpretations of the environmentalist and state debates; one might accept the framework but reject the claim about the insufficiency of both positions, arguing in favor of one of them (Merleau-Ponty's *Phenomenology of Perception* comes to mind); one might seek a perspective on nature and the state that breaks from the Faith-Enlightenment terms of debate. The last is the aspiration of this chapter. I cannot guarantee that such a perspective will be superior to established ones, but its appeal lies partly in the fact that its promise has not yet disappointed.

2. Michel Foucault, "The Order of Discourse," in *Untying the Text*, ed. Robert Young (Boston: Routledge and Kegan Paul, 1981), p. 67.

3. Michel Foucault, *The History of Sexuality*, vol. 1 (New York: Vintage, 1980), p. 142.

4. Charles Taylor, "Connolly, Foucault, and Truth," *Political Theory* 13, August 1985, p. 7.

5. See, for example, *Discipline and Punish* (New York: Vintage, 1979) and *Madness and Civilization* (New York: Vintage, 1973).

6. Foucault, *Sexuality*, pp. 152–53.

7. Foucault, *Sexuality*, p. 156.

8. Foucault, *Sexuality*, pp. 144–45.

9. See also William Connolly, "Taylor, Foucault and Otherness," *Political Theory* 13, August 1985.

10. Michel Foucault, "What Is Enlightenment?," in *The Foucault Reader*, ed. Paul Rabinow (New York: Pantheon, 1984), p. 41.

11. Foucault, "What Is Enlightenment?," p. 41.

12. Michel Foucault, *Power/Knowledge*, ed. Colin Gordon (New York: Pantheon, 1977), p. 138.

13. See, for example, E. F. Schumacher, "Buddhist Economics," in *Small Is Beautiful* (New York: Harper and Row, 1975); William Ophuls, "Leviathan or Oblivion," in *Toward a Steady-State Economy*, ed. Herman Daly (San Francisco: W. H. Freeman, 1973); Charles Taylor, "The Politics of the Steady-State," in *Beyond Industrial Growth*, ed. Abraham Rotstein (Toronto: Univ. of Toronto Press, 1976); Warren Johnson, *Muddling toward Frugality* (San Francisco: Sierra Club Books, 1978).

14. Foucault, "What Is Enlightenment?," p. 46.

15. Friedrich Nietzsche, *The Gay Science*, trans. Walter Kaufmann (New York: Vintage, 1974), p. 232.

INDEX